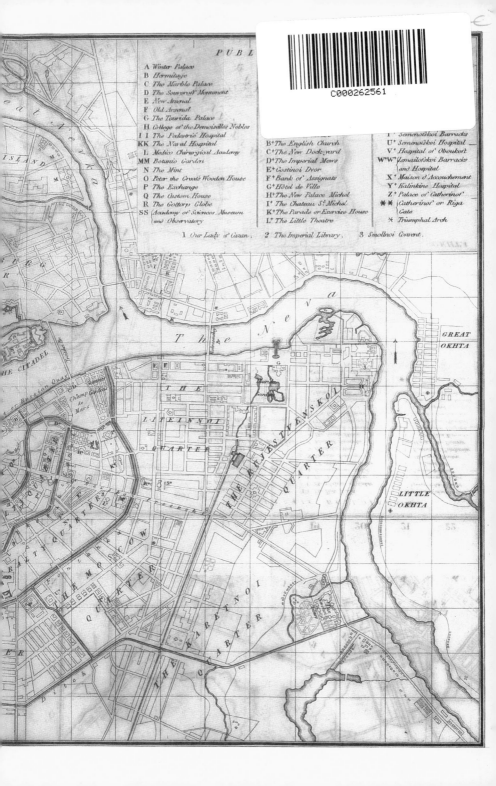

A VISIT TO
ST PETERSBURG

1824-1825

———

Cornélie de Wassenaer

Translated and edited by

IGOR VINOGRADOFF

MICHAEL RUSSELL

© A.R.A. Hobson 1994

First published in Great Britain 1994
by Michael Russell (Publishing) Ltd
Wilby Hall, Wilby, Norwich NR16 2JP

Printed and bound in Great Britain
by Biddles Ltd, Guildford and King's Lynn

Typeset in Bembo
by The Typesetting Bureau, Wimborne, Dorset

Contents

Acknowledgements

Grateful thanks are due, on behalf of the late Igor Vinogradoff and the publishers, to Count Alfred Solms, the owner of Cornélie de Wassenaer's journal, for permission to publish this translation; to Professor Coenraad Tamse of the University of Groningen for much valuable assistance; to Mrs Noël Blakiston for her introduction to Professor Tamse; to Mr Peter Collingridge for assimilating research on the notes and for locating the cover illustration; to Mr Anthony Hobson for further valuable assistance; and to Dr J. S. G. Simmons of All Souls College, Oxford, who most generously devoted much time to the final annotation of the text and the completion of Igor Vinogradoff's index.

Introduction

Marie Cornélie de Wassenaer (1799–1850), the author of this journal, appeared quiet and unassuming. She was nevertheless the greatest heiress in the Netherlands – although this may have seemed paltry in the overweening world of St Petersburg where the courtiers chose to sneer at small bourgeois states.

Her mother, née Margarita Alewijn of a patrician banking family from Amsterdam, had died when Cornélie was one year old, and her father, the last Count of Wassenaer, whom she hardly knew, had died when she was only thirteen, leaving her a Countess of the Holy Roman Empire, Gravin van Wassenaer (already a flourishing suburb of The Hague), Baroness of Lage, and Lady of nine other properties in Gelderland and Overijssel (Opdam, Twickel, Hensbroek, Spierdijk, Wogmeer, Zuidwijk, Kerhem, Weldam and Olidam). She inherited a huge banking fortune and with it a large town house, which she lost little time in selling to the Royal House of Orange-Nassau as one of their palaces. Her pedigree stretched back to the twelfth century and included the 'Opdam' of the Duke of Dorset's famous song, who had died in glorious battle against the English fleet in 1665 and is commemorated in the Grote Kerk in The Hague.

Cornélie's journals and letters reveal her feelings of loneliness amid her great possessions, and explain her passionate devotion to her stepmother, her father's third wife, née Wilhelmina van Heeckeren van Kell, whom he had married in 1805, and whom Cornélie always called her mother. She was similarly devoted to her van Heeckeren cousins Agatha (1801–62) and Julia (1802–82), her stepmother's nieces, who lived at Ruurlo, close to Cornélie's country house at Twickel. She wrote regular fortnightly letters to them throughout her Russian odyssey and it was these letters that helped her later to write up the journal.

Some of her tastes were settled: she loved music passionately, from Rossini to gypsy music, and even the organ. She also loved the theatre at all levels, felt frustration at not seeing Talma in Paris in 1820, enjoyed the childish amateur performances at Gatchina, and although she did not think much of the St Petersburg French actors or their silly little plays, saw them frequently all the same. She liked romantic fiction and romanticised history such as Scott's novels and the lives of Joan of Arc and Mlle de la Vallière. She also admired the romantic landscapes of the Rhineland and Thuringia, and even the picturesque lakes and forests of East Prussia and the Baltic provinces of Russia, though driving through them gave her days and nights of tribulation. She detested politics and political discussion – which was something she was spared in St Petersburg.

What displeased her, as an heiress, was the kind concern of Dutch gossips that she might fall victim to a fortune hunter. That some were casting around her in St Petersburg was obvious, but she was quite determined to ignore them. Her letters to her cousins make it clear that she watched other people's romances and marriages with ardent interest but, however she might dream, felt sure that she would remain single herself. Mrs (later Lady) Cartwright, wife of the English Secretary at The Hague, records this in her diary in 1830.

The fact was that Cornélie was mis-shapen ('difformée' is the word used by Mrs Cartwright; she may have had a curvature of the spine) and, though her face and personality were charming and she received affection from innumerable friends, she was convinced that no man could possibly want to marry her except for her fortune. Mrs Cartwright liked her, as most people did, and thought her wrong. Eventually Cornélie, perhaps in partial compromise, married in 1831 Charles van Heeckeren, the younger brother of Agnes and Julia, who was ten years her junior. It was a childless marriage which secured her properties for the people she loved, though none of them passed, as she would also have liked, to Wassenaers of another branch.

She had been brought up to know everything a young lady of her position should know. She was a pious member of the Dutch Reformed Church, but was prepared to go to Lutheran and even Russian Orthodox services – though never Roman Catholic ones – as a matter of duty, though she did not count the Russian Orthodox, however fine the singing, as a religious service. French was her natural language, but she could also speak Dutch and German (not all the aristocrats of the Netherlands understood Dutch). She painted with enthusiasm when at home and played the piano adequately, often hiring a piano if she found herself somewhere without one.

She had travelled a good deal before her epic journey to St Petersburg – in Germany where her stepmother accompanied the exiled House of Orange, and to Paris, first in 1814 (which has not been recorded in her journals) and again in 1820, a city then full of Napoleon's unfinished buildings. She was taken over Rheims Cathedral by an old man who had witnessed the coronation of Louis XVI, and at St Germain was shown the lift by which Louis XIV had visited his mistress Louise de la Vallière. This satisfied her taste for the romance of history, although her passion for the stage was unfulfilled, as she was desperately disappointed not to have seen Talma act. A total contrast was her later trip to the Paris of Louis-Philippe in 1834, with its brilliant gas-lit shops, theatres, famous restaurants, and the newly acquired Venus de Milo in the Louvre. Cornélie visited the theatre thirty times, and her husband Charles fifty, during their three-month stay, seeing Grisi in opera, Taglioni in ballet, and actresses such as Mlle Mars on the dramatic stage.

In 1836 she visited England, which was enjoyable in a different way. London was disappointing: the van Heeckerens knew no one, the Houses of Parliament had just been burnt down, the court of William IV was barely visible and mediocre, and the royal palaces much inferior to the noble houses Cornélie had seen on the Continent. Their tour around the country, on the other hand, impressed her greatly, especially the enormous palaces of the aristocracy and their congeners – Blenheim, Warwick, Stowe, Chatsworth, Eaton, Longleat, Wilton and so on. Chatsworth made the friendliest impression. She was welcomed at the door by two amiable bulldogs, which had been bred by the Bachelor (the 6th) Duke. Cornélie made her one and only journey in a steam train between Manchester and Liverpool, but saw railway construction everywhere. England's Industrial Revolution was in full swing and she was suitably impressed by Birmingham and by Brunel's tunnel underneath the Thames.

Her trips in Germany and to Paris had been private, unlike her journey to Russia as a maid of honour to the court of the House of Orange-Nassau. They had given her little experience of men, let alone the blasé courtiers and generals of St Petersburg at a time when she was still a shy provincial girl. Her great inheritance and ancestry made no difference. Nurtured in frugal self-denying Calvinism, she could not be attracted or corrupted by the grandeur of St Petersburg. Living in the modest economy of Twickel, she grudged the cost of postage to her beloved Netherlands and preferred official couriers who were slower but cost nothing. It was the same instinctive semi-religious thrift that made her sell unwanted court dresses in St Petersburg when she required more summer clothes for Pavlovsk; she called it 'faire la Juive'. (Her stepmother tried to do the same on her departure but found the old clothes dealer would not buy.) Mrs Cartwright noticed her torn and dirty gloves in 1830 and said her stinginess was proverbial. This though both Cornélie and her stepmother could dress like peacocks on great occasions.

Her chief love was her home and when away she was morbidly homesick for her native Overijssel, especially Twickel, a moated castle full of family portraits and superb

French furniture. She dreamed constantly of its simple familiar sights and sounds – the cocks, the cows, the swallows – especially when the changeable weather of St Petersburg depressed her. Her regular correspondence with her cousins Agatha and Julia van Heeckeren kept her homesickness alive. All sorts of things reminded her of them and of Ruurlo, making her long for home – the River Rhine because it flowed down to Holland, the moon because it was their moon too, the Frankfurt fashion journals which they also saw, an English shawl because her first such shawl had been bought with Agatha in Germany, the music of Weber, Rossini and Dalayrac and many waltzes and romantic melodies which she heard everywhere from Germany to St Petersburg and which both kept up her courage and moved her to tears.

Part schoolroom sophistication, part adolescent naïveté, she was easily shocked – by the Italian nudes in picture galleries or by the ballerinas' costumes. She loved sentimental stories and was immature in her emotions. It was no doubt this prolonged adolescence that made her feel at sea in the male St Petersburg world of Tolstoy's *War and Peace*. Sukhtelen and Paolucci, Chernyshev and Miloradovich, and the mysterious Emperor himself are only some of the Tolstoy characters Cornélie actually met, not to mention the actual conspirators against the Emperor Paul. She felt, and was, a schoolgirl among these formidable personages and judged them by schoolgirl standards. Miloradovich, the man of fifty battles, was dismissed as the 'Nightingale' because he talked so much, and Paolucci, one of Alexander's cosmopolitan fighting men, as an entertaining flirt who made her fellow maid of honour Pauline Comtesse d'Oultremont roar with laughter. Chernyshev, the skilled intelligence agent who scored off Napoleon and became Russia's Minister of War, she thought chiefly remarkable for his vanity.

On the other hand her innocence made her fit quite naturally into the Dowager Empress Maria Fedorovna's female schoolroom court, with its games room at Gatchina, amateur theatricals and blind man's buff, reading aloud and guessing games, visiting 'dames de classe' from the Smol'nyi Institute, the boarding school for girls started by Catherine the Great, and the handsome maids of honour at Gatchina and Pavlovsk. Cornélie's sense of fun and nimble verbal wit made her a welcome member of this circle, though she was bored by the childish romping games and sinister or dissolute memories of the aged survivors of the reigns of Catherine the Great and Paul made her uneasy.

She came to feel deeply for the ordered beauty of the capital and its majestic palaces and regretted leaving them; she felt 'my little person' to be out of place amidst these splendours but this made her specially observant of every detail in a totally strange world. She could not be expected to understand the enormous transformation of Europe since her birth. She saw immediate objects much larger than life, as little people do when they look up at monuments. This gives her journal its charm and authenticity.

The journal of her trip to Russia and her stay in St Petersburg was written in fluent cosmopolitan French, the language of the time among the European upper class. This, like the other four diaries of her travels to Paris in 1820 and 1834, and to England in 1836, is copied out in her hand in seven small notebooks, each of 180 pages, and is faithfully preserved at Weldam Castle in the Eastern Netherlands by Cornélie's eventual heir, Count Alfred Solms.

In her journal Cornéie recorded her experiences while accompanying the Prince and Princess of Orange-Nassau on an official visit to Russia to the court of Emperor Alexander I and his family at St Petersburg in 1824-5.

The Princess of Orange was born Grand Duchess Anna Pavlovna (1795-1865), the daughter of the Emperor Paul and Maria Fedorovna, and the youngest sister of Alexander I. She was married in 1816 to William, Prince of Orange-Nassau, but she never lost her feeling of importance as a Russian

Grand Duchess and never wavered in her creed of strict legitimism, unlike her versatile husband, to whom she always remained loyal. She was popular in Holland and the Northern Provinces because, unlike most royal personages of the period, she bothered to learn Dutch. Her dowry of jewels was superb and symbolised her status.

William, her husband, was born in 1792 and spent his formative years in exile in Germany and England from 1795 until the downfall of Napoleon in 1814. His governess during this time was Cornélie's stepmother. Educated at the Prussian Cadet Corps and Christ Church, Oxford, and the Duke of Wellington's ADC during the Peninsular War, he thought in princely French and spoke Dutch with a German or English accent. Thanks to his command of the Dutch Corps at Quatre Bras and Waterloo, where he was wounded, he became immensely popular in the Netherlands. Constantly in disagreement with the policies of his father, King William I of Holland, he is said to have changed his political views eight times. Flirtatious and captivating, he always kept the devotion of his wife and remained great friends with his brothers-in-law, the Emperors Alexander I and Nicholas I, whom he resembled in their passion for constant restless travel. He became King William II of Holland on his father's abdication in 1840 and died in 1849.

Cornélie went to Russia as maid of honour to the Princess of Orange-Nassau. She was accompanied by her stepmother, the future Queen's lady-in-waiting and Mistress of the Robes, who, because of her earlier services to the House of Orange-Nassau, the Prince always introduced as his second mother. She won the devotion of Cornélie and of her nieces Agatha and Julia through her strength of character and her ability to make them laugh and share their jokes.

The van Heeckeren family is remembered in Russia to this day for the sordid part that Baron Ludwig Heeckeren tot Enkhuize en Beverwaard, the Dutch minister in St Petersburg from 1823 to 1837, who rates many minor references in

Cornélie's journal, played in provoking Pushkin to his fatal duel with the ambassador's French adopted son, d'Anthès, in 1837. Pushkin is not mentioned in the journal as he had been banished to his estates at Mikhailovskoe during the time Cornélie was in the capital.

Cornélie was also accompanied by a fellow maid of honour, Comtesse Pauline d'Oultremont (1793-1852). Pauline, as she is called throughout the journal, was from a rich noble family in the Bishopric of Liège where her great-uncle had been Prince Bishop from 1763 to 1771. Her eldest sister, Henriette (1792-1864), became the second, morganatic, wife of King William I in 1840, a marriage that forced him to abdicate – the Dutch would not tolerate a royal consort who was both a Belgian and a Roman Catholic. Cornélie remained great friends with Pauline and her other sister, Charlotte (1795-1874), neither of whom married, despite the fact that they became Belgian subjects and remained Roman Catholics. She saw much of them during her visit to Paris in 1834.

The Dutch travellers went to Russia by way of Weimar to visit the Princess's sister, the Grand Duchess Maria Pavlovna (1786-1859), who was universally popular and sometimes called 'the pearl of the Romanovs'. She had married Charles Frederick, Crown Prince of Saxe-Weimar (1783-1853), in 1804. He supported his father in his difficult balancing act between Napoleon and the Allied powers from 1806 until 1813, but was singularly unfitted for a role as patron of writers such as Goethe in a Duchy famous for its leading place in German culture. Charles Frederick succeeded as Duke of Saxe-Weimar in 1828. His ignorance and malapropisms made him Cornélie's favourite butt.

From Weimar the travellers proceeded to St Petersburg. The Emperor was coming to the end of his reign still haunted by an overwhelming feeling of guilt over the death of his father, Paul. Paul was born in 1754, married Sophia Dorothea of the junior Montbéliard branch of the ducal House of Württemberg, who took the name Maria Fedorovna, and succeeded his mother, Catherine II the Great, in 1796. He detested his mother and reversed all her policies. In little over four years he made a caricature of the autocracy and bitterly antagonised the entire upper ranks of his official ruling class, both military and civil. This was decisive, because the wave of loathing included the officers of the Guard, by whom the poor, insufferable, schizophrenic despot was removed on 24 March 1801. Alexander had had previous knowledge of the plot to make his father abdicate, but had thought that his life would be spared.

Paul's wife, Maria Fedorovna (1755-1828), had supported his many eccentricities, having been brought up in a family that had its fair share of brutes and bullies. She herself had been difficult and despotic to her own ladies in her earlier days, but had mellowed after her husband's assassination into the benevolent matriarch of Cornélie's visit, who spent her time in philanthropic works, founding educational and charitable institutions. This did not mean that she had lost her strong but carefully veiled dislike for Alexander's wife, over whom she took precedence in all ceremonies, due to a novel law of Paul's which gave pre-eminence to the Dowager over the reigning Empress. As the Dowager Empress after his death, she chose to forget the humiliating rudeness with which she had been treated in his last days, and built up a cult of veneration, bordering on worship, for the 'martyred' Emperor.

So the court into which the Wassenaers made their entry on 10 October 1824 was dominated by the Dowager Empress, who had imposed a schoolroom routine and a rigorous etiquette, combined with massive grandeur that was always taken for granted. The Dowager rarely saw the Emperor and his wife, partly because of their ill-health, but largely because the unapproachable Emperor in this last year of his reign was taken up with his devotions and had little time for anything else but paperwork, inspections, solitary drives and incessant travels across his empire. The court lived in sublime indifference to the ordinary people and it is life at court that Cornélie described. The memory of Paul's death was preserved by Maria Fedorovna's monuments and ceremonies, of which everyone in the palaces was constantly aware, not least Cornélie, who could not get over her frequent meetings with one of the conspirators, General Uvarov, the commander of the Guard Corps, popular, successful, genial, and favoured by the Emperor.

Alexander I, born in 1777, passed through every phase of liberalism until 1820, when he became fixed in opposition to any thought of relaxation or reform. This in itself would not have affected the vast masses of his subjects, but his refusal to give the smallest backing to the Greek uprising of 1821 against their Turkish rulers was quite another matter. It seemed a grievous sin to many Orthodox believers at all levels and this affected the Emperor deeply. At the same time he never lost his unique charm (strongly attested even by such an irritably critical writer as L. N. Tolstoy) and his power to inspire love among his family and intimates, if not his ministers. He remained the 'angel' to his wife, family and courtiers, and it was he who left Cornélie and Pauline spellbound, even though they rarely caught a glimpse of him. Cornélie could not fail to know about the sinister event which dominated Alexander's reign and personality, the murder of his father, and refers to this Oedipus tragedy so frequently as to sound a melancholy refrain throughout her journal. It is this that explains the gentle monarch's suspiciousness and obsession with parade-ground order, inherited from his father, as well as his extraordinary devotion to Count Arakcheev, whose only merit was his much-belauded loyalty.

Alexander had been married in October 1793, at the instigation of his grandmother Catherine the Great, to Princess Louise of Baden (1779-1826), who took the Orthodox name of Elizaveta Alexeevna. Alexander was sixteen and she just fourteen. During the reign of the Emperor Paul she was treated by her mother-in-law, the Empress Maria Fedorovna, with rudeness bordering on physical roughness. Elizaveta Alexeevna had not forgotten, and an antipathy remained between the two

Empresses at the time of Cornélie's visit. She bore Alexander two girls (one of whom she called 'Little Mouse'). Both died before the age of two. Although the Emperor had been unfaithful before, the Empress intensely resented Alexander's Polish-born mistress Maria Antonovna Naryshkin, née Chetvertinskii, a liaison which lasted many years and produced children, but was deeply sympathetic when all the children died. During his last year, however, the Emperor and Empress spent what she called 'their second honeymoon'.

Alexander had, as well as sisters, three brothers. Constantine (1779-1831) was Governor of the Grand Duchy of Poland and lived in Warsaw with his second, morganatic, wife, and had secretly renounced his succession to the throne. Nicholas (1796-1855), the future Emperor Nicholas I, was married to the beautiful Princess Charlotte of Prussia, known as Grand Duchess Alexandrine. Nicholas, though charming to his family, was a stickler for discipline. This and his coldness had made him very unpopular with the Army, especially the Guards regiments, and his wife was not remarkable for her tact. The youngest of the brothers, Michael (1798-1849), was like his brother Nicholas a military martinet, but famous for his puns and for his caustic wit. He was married to Princess Charlotte of Württemberg (1807-73), known as the Grand Duchess Elena Pavlovna and the object of much real popular affection in Russia, unlike her father and uncle, King William I of Württemberg, who made themselves detested for their arrogance and selfish ruthlessness. The only exception to the unison of her admirers was her husband, who had no use for prodigies of culture and good works, however perfect; their marriage was not a success.

Cornélie had some notion of what lay behind this multi-faceted and brilliant court in the vast and formidable empire, where Metternich's verbose lecturing dictated foreign policy, and day-to-day decisions on home affairs were left to provincial satraps. Alexander's favourite undertaking, 'military colonies', originally started with the most humane intentions to settle soldiers' families on the land, were brutally transformed into a form of militarised labour by his loathsome underling, Count Arakcheev. Cornélie knew something of what was meant by military colonies, fortunately limited to Novgorod and part of the Ukraine. When the Prince of Orange and Chernyshev returned from these grim places with optimistic tales, she already knew the truth about them from the servants, who were better informed on such matters. Her passing references to such things, rarely recorded elsewhere, give a dimension to her journal above that of a mere court chronicle.

Cornélie was no Custine; she was not writing a lampoon or trying to 'kick the sea', to use Grand Duke Michael's phrase. Hers is an unvarnished account of life among great beauties and people she liked more and more in an atmosphere she sometimes found oppressive. She pokes mild fun at her 'Highnesses', notably the Prince of Saxe-Weimar, occasionally the Dowager Empress and even her own Princess of Orange. She tells of her girlish admiration for the mysterious, agreeable, isolated Emperor, the one hero in her journal. Her complete aversion to politics in any form makes it all the more convincing as a true account of court life in St Petersburg, with all its sinister background noises as well as feasts. Many things bore and disgust Cornélie in Russia – the stinking palace corridors, the monotonous food, the dull evening parties, the old powdered ladies, the hours of tedious routine and of waiting on an unpredictable princess, the unaccountable winter, the occasional revolting sights or anecdotes.

One source of these anecdotes was the Hogguer family. They were a rich cosmopolitan banking family of Swiss origin with connections in Sweden and France, who had settled in Holland during the eighteenth century. One had become burgomaster of Amsterdam and president of the Netherlands Bank. His brother, Jan Willem Baron Hogguer (1755-1838), was the Dutch minister in St Petersburg from 1791 to 1795, when he resigned and entered the Russian service. He became governor of Courland and in 1800 married a Russian wife, Anna Alexandrovna Polyanskii. She was the daughter of the Emperor Peter III's unlucky mistress Elizaveta Romanovna Vorontsov, who had been married off to a Polyanskii. Baron Hogguer and his wife had three daughters, but none of the family was received at court. They may have borne a grudge in consequence, and it may account for the pleasure they took in spreading horror stories. Cornélie recorded them, but may not have believed them all. She became very friendly with the daughters, especially the eldest, Betty, who married Baron Alexander Kazimirovich Meyendorff (1798-1865), a younger brother of the celebrated diplomat. Cornélie saw a lot of them in Paris as late as 1834, but eventually lost touch with them.

What made Cornélie like her ten-month stay and look back on it with enough pleasure to write it all down? Above all, the universal kindness she encountered, not only from the ladies, 'Cochette' (Mlle Kochetov), Princess Khilkov, old Countess Lieven, even Maria Fedorovna for all her weaknesses, but also from the men she had at first most feared. Next, set against the long periods of boredom, the marvellous ceremonies and entertainments on a colossal scale in magical surroundings – the superb church singing, the Blessing of the Waters, the White Ball with 10,000 candles, the Winter Palace Masquerade with more than 20,000 guests, the review on the Champ de Mars with more than 40,000 troops. Last but not least, the exquisite beauty of the palaces outside the city, Pavlovsk, the park at Tsarskoe Selo, the great fountains playing at Peterhof.

The Journey

The little cavalcade left Brussels in the pouring rain on 8 September 1824. There were two light carriages for the Prince and Princess, another light carriage and two heavy berlines for their suite, and a whole string of other conveyances for their servants – cooks, a farrier and saddler, maids and footmen, with the lighter luggage which had not been sent in advance. Speeds being very different, the convoy did not drive in unison: the gentlemen sometimes drove day and night, but the best the whole cavalcade was able to do, allowing for three extended stops of nine nights in all, was some 1,400 English miles in twenty-four days' driving. The Prince was later able to complete the whole distance in ten days and eighteen hours in the following mid-March when the roads were covered with smooth snow which made sleighing very fast.

This was the old Europe of the Restoration. Macadamised roads hardly existed east of Leipzig, after which bumpy paved roads alternated with appalling forest tracks through sand; the passenger steamship route had yet to be established from St Petersburg to Lübeck, and extended railway travel was some thirty years in the future. Hence the grim conditions, where the better roads might be fast if dangerous, but postilions often had to struggle through deep mud or cope with tree trunks or the roots of pine trees on dreadful tracks, maximum speeds could often be as little as four miles per hour, and inns did not exist outside provincial capitals.

Moreover, Europe was politically still the Europe of the Vienna Settlement. The Prince of Orange-Nassau acted for his father, King William I of the United Netherlands, as viceroy in his southern (Belgian) provinces. His entire suite was Belgian with the exception of Cornélie de Wassenaer, as maid of honour, and her stepmother as Mistress of the Robes to the Princess. The inns and roads in western

*Germany were good, but everywhere in that rich country divided into
numerous independent states there were customs barriers and different currencies, which killed trade, pauperised the peasants and
constantly delayed the progress of the ordinary traveller. One of
the tangible advantages of travelling with a prince and princess,
Cornélie remarked, was to escape at least the customs barriers. Instead of taking a more direct route to St Petersburg they travelled to
Weimar to spend five nights with the Princess's elder sister, the
Crown Princess of Saxe-Weimar.*

*The journey was the eventful prologue to Cornélie's stay in St
Petersburg, a destination so desirable because it was so distant and
difficult to reach − on the same latitude as the Orkney Islands with
what seemed to Western Europeans an Arctic climate; 'Ville superbe,
que fais-tu là?', as one perceptive traveller remarked. Cornélie
laughed off some of her experiences on the road, which Dr Granville,
making the same journey three years later, compared for difficulty
with crossing the Sierra Morena, the Alps or the Pyrenees.*

*As far as Weimar the journey was a stately progress which only
claimed one victim − Comtesse d'Oultremont, their hostess at Duras,
who had such nervous cramps the night before their arrival that she
was too ill to receive them. A Russian Grand Duchess was an
object of considerable awe. In Frankfurt-am-Main on 12 September
Cornélie records:*

Audiences succeeded one another without a break and we
finally sat down to table without bothering about M. Grün, our
minister in Frankfurt, or his wife. We had hardly swallowed
our soup when the Landgrave of Hessen–Homburg and his wife
sent to ask at what hour they could pay homage to our
Highnesses. They were asked to return in an hour's time. . .

*The Landgrave was, no doubt, a minor ruler, but a reigning prince
for all that and married to a daughter of the King of England. There-
after the journal becomes somewhat repetitious in its account of the
journey, with Cornélie becoming increasingly homesick, suffering fits
of overpowering shyness and being subjected to court duties for the
first time in her life as well as a good deal of obligatory sightseeing.*

[23]

The court of Weimar, with its rigorous etiquette and constant changes of dress, was a useful introduction to the court of St Petersburg. Cornélie was terrified among the courtiers, none of whom she knew.

I followed Pauline like a shadow and consoled myself with the thought that I should go in last. The reigning Grand Duchess is a figure of the Ancien Régime; she is tall and dignified, and they say she showed a lot of character in difficult times. Her daughter-in-law is like her sister, our Princess, though a little stouter, with much charm and kindness in her manners. The Grand Duke is a fat little man with rather vulgar ways and an undistiguished record.[1] His son is very ugly, both in voice and looks. The whole court treated us with great politeness. At table I found myself next to a very civil lady who talked a little too much; I took her for a maid of honour but later found that she was under-governess to the Princesses; she is called Mlle Sylvestre.

Thursday, September 16th. This is a terrible day with constant changing of dresses, exits, entrances, not two minutes to oneself. We had to call on all the ladies of both courts, beginning with the Countess Fritsch, the Princess Maria's Mistress of the Robes, a woman of much rather bitter wit. . . The most agreeable time was when we heard the famous Hummel[2] show off his real talent on the piano; he took up the melody 'Tanti palpiti' [by Rossini] and used it for the prettiest variations I have ever heard in my life. When he had stopped playing I slid out of the exalted sanctuary and found Mlle

---

[1] Grand Duke Charles Augustus of Saxe-Weimar (1775-1828), the patron of Goethe and Schiller, had been caught in the dilemma of so many minor German princes when Prussia broke with Napoleon in 1806. He had started in the inglorious campaign of Jena as a Prussian general, had surrendered at Auerstadt, become a general in the French army and reverted to the Allies in 1813. The accepted version, fathered by Napoleon, was that his Duchy had been saved for him by his brave Grand Duchess.

[2] The German composer Johann Nepomuk Hummel (1778-1837), once an infant prodigy, had known Mozart and was considered Beethoven's rival at the piano. He was the conductor of the court orchestra at Weimar.

Sylvestre talking about music with M. de Bavay. She gave a very powerful description of [Weber's] *Der Freischütz*, which I longed to hear. From music they passed on to tolerance in religious matters and M. de Bavay jokingly called us heretics and damned souls but simultaneously assured us he could never believe that all non-Catholics were shut out from Heaven. Mlle Sylvestre [no doubt of Huguenot origin] bluntly told him she thought anyone who believed this mad.

I was put next to the Grand Duke Michael's ADC, M. Kavelin, at supper; his forbidding Kalmuk face did not give me a pleasant notion of the Russian countenance. He told me that his master forces him to travel; they are always on the move and he has reckoned that in five years' time he will have been made to cover 40,000 versts or rather more than 27,000 miles.

Friday, September 17th. We had a visit from M. Vitzthum, who is Chamberlain to the junior court. He is a very agreeable talker and we made friends quickly, Pauline having known him in the years 1814/15 in Brussels. In those days he was an elegant, excellent dancer and all the Brussels ladies raved about the 'Little Saxon', as they called him. It turned out that Mama had known him even earlier in Berlin as a page and we laughed hugely when we discovered that the 'Little Page', the 'Little Saxon' and the 'Little Chamberlain' were one and the same person. He did not paint a very pleasant picture of the court of St Petersburg and we also heard that the Weimar court had not been a success in Russia. We took courage with the reflection that, given a little kindness and politeness on our part, they could hardly quarrel with us.

Saturday, September 18th. We had to wait a very long time for dinner because the Grand Duke of Saxe-Weimar was giving the Prince of Orange-Nassau and the Grand Duke Nicholas of Russia the pleasure of a stag hunt. In the meantime we made conversation and the Prince of Weimar did his best to make his contribution. In talking of our gentlemen he spoke of 'M. de Baveux'[3] and Mama was so carried away with

3 'Slobberer', a mistake for 'Bavay'.

[25]

the desire to laugh that she had a sort of convulsion. This made the Princess Maria think she was in a shivering fit and the open windows were upsetting her. There was a rush to shut them that made me laugh as well. . . My neighbours at dinner started talking about the Romans. M. Vitzthum would not tolerate ending any proper name in '-us'; he maintained one must say 'Luculle' and not 'Lucullus'. I asked my neighbour *sotto voce* what he would do with 'Crassus'. She repeated this out loud and everyone laughed and made so much noise that I withdrew into myself and took no more part. . . Countess Fritsch took us to the theatre where they were giving a performance of Spontini's *Fernand Cortez*. The court box is big but I was disconcerted by a row of empty chairs in front of us reserved for absent Highnesses, behind which we respectfully had to sit. One of them was occupied by the Prince of Hesse-Philipsthal-Barchfeld, a general in the Russian service, whom we had dined with every day. He had lost a leg fighting against the French and this proof of courage, together with his noble and agreeable expression, impresses everyone who sees him. As a member of a reigning house he had to sit in the front row but pushed his chair back so as to be almost abreast of us. The Prince of Saxe-Weimar is not strong in history, not even the latest by the look of it. Talking of the Prince of Hesse and his wooden leg to Pauline, he remarked to her 'That's what comes of fighting against the Turks.'

Sunday, September 19th. We dressed for dinner at the Senior Court and made our curtseys in the usual manners, first to our Princess, then to the Princess Maria and last to the reigning Grand Duchess. . . After dinner we took leave of the Princess Maria before she went back to the Belvedere where she lives. . . We had not finished yet. We had to reappear at eight o'clock for the Drawing Room the Grand Duchess holds every Sunday, to take leave of her. This lasted a good hour. We saw all the fine people of Weimar, including a good many English, who are said to stay there to improve their German as well as possibly to economise. The pages offered tea to everyone. At last

[26]

the Grand Duchess sat down at her card table under a canopy with two pages behind her, and we hastened to beat a retreat.

The travellers left Weimar the following day. It was after Leipzig that the scene began to change, with grinding drives only relieved by comic incidents and the ability to laugh at them. They had been warned that after Leipzig they would miss nothing by travelling to St Petersburg with their eyes shut, but no mention was made of the state of the roads.

Monday, September 20th. Near Torgau we came upon the luggage van unharnessed in the middle of the road and the saddler pacing up and down beside it gloomily while the horses rested; they had been dropping with fatigue. . . So to avoid the deep sand the postilions followed side tracks bumping over the pine roots which shook us up most dreadfully. There were five postilions in all; the three who were on foot urged the horses on with such peculiar shouts that one might have thought oneself amidst a band of robbers; their grotesque appearance made us laugh continually. One wore white trousers and a little blue jacket with a red and white cap which made him look like a Turk; his companion was dressed in a long frock coat with a huge pipe in his mouth, whom we called 'the Persian'.

This was a rarely travelled route and those who went that way attracted much attention. The party reached Lüben, where they were to sleep, at half past midnight on 22 September, after twenty hours of continuous driving except for short stops to eat. 'Mama had undressed the Princess and put her to bed. Her maids had not arrived!' After Lüben a distant stag hunt in the forest full of splendid pines and small lakes set Cornélie and Pauline inventing a romance. A handsome huntsman, shooting a stag, wounds one of the girls and naturally falls in love with her. The obligatory happy ending is the marriage of the desperate hero and the wounded girl. Such was the sentimental stuff of their dreams which helped to keep them going on their way.

Three nights' 'rest' at Deutsch Krone on 24-26 September epitomised the joys of travel in eastern Germany. As there was no inn the Princess occupied the postmaster's little salon; the ladies had

*his bedroom, which was also the dining room for all the suite, with
the maids all crammed into another small room and the footmen
eating in the passage. A little cat provided their first amusement by
hiding in Pauline's bed and waking her with its mewing under her
pillow. The walls were black with flies and Cornélie was woken by
them promenading over her face. Fly traps were of little use and
warning placards on the tables were just another joke provided by the
gentlemen. When the Princess dined with them and tried to sit on
Cornélie's feather bed, she nearly disappeared in an abyss and
furnished them with just a little more discreet amusement.*

*The Prince arrived and took them for a walk. 'Deutsch Krone was
the ugliest place; its roads great piles of filth, replenished by the
steady to and fro of geese, cows, pigs, goats and sheep − the great
majority of the population of the town.' Jews were more numerous
than gentiles among the human beings, and they solemnly watched
(it being the Sabbath) the Prince and his courtiers set out, 'accompanied by all the ragamuffins in the town' and ushered home by the
inevitable geese. There was tea and écarté in the evening to give this
dreary halt a touch of civilisation.*

*Thence to the Prussian frontier meant five days of obstinate bump-
ing through the pines and sand with only a small stretch of pretty
countryside between the estuaries of the Vistula and Nogat and one
great spectacle, the Castle of the Knights at Marienburg (now Mal-
bork), to ease the tedium. On Saturday 12 October they crossed a
little river accompanied by a Cossack guard and were at last in the
Polish kingdom of the Emperor Alexander of Russia. It was twenty-
four days since they had left Brussels.*

Russia

October 1824

Saturday, October 2nd. From Gumbinen to Vladislavovo we were very much bumped. A little river, guarded by Cossacks, marks the frontier here between Prussia and Russian Poland. At Vladislavovo they drove us to the police officer's, who received us at the carriage door, and as I was the first to get out he gave me his hand to conduct me into the house, where he presented his wife. She could speak nothing but Polish but made many curtseys and uttered a few words in German. Though unable to converse with us, she kept coming back every moment and seemed to think politeness did not allow her to leave us alone. We had a lot of trouble getting a basin to wash in; finally a tin one was produced and we had to put our six hands in it and dry them on the same towel.

We were to dine at the priest's house where the table had been laid for dinner and I was exceedingly surprised to see our hostess come in with us; for a moment I supposed that both she and a Cossack officer and several other people were going to honour us with their company for dinner. I soon realised, however, that the lady had only come to help the priest with dinner preparations. The good curate, an old man of venerable appearance, and his servant Ignace, followed by our hostess, ran about continually in search of vinegar or a little mustard. The Prince and Princess were late in arriving, so we remained idle spectators of the curate's preparations, our only distraction being the sight of utterly wretched people crowded around the house – cripples of every kind covered with sheepskins and with their faces hidden by manes of dirty hair.

At last we heard a carriage. It was the Grand Duke Michael on his way to Warsaw. He sat down with us, asked about Their Highnesses' plans and, finding we could tell him nothing, complimented us on our excellent discipline and on the obedience with which we allowed ourselves to be dragged about. He was accompanied by an ADC called Bibikov with eyes and hair blacker than jet; Pauline called him the 'handsomest of the blacks'. At last our Highnesses arrived and their joy at finding Michael was immense. After dinner and tea we returned home in the lovely moonlight. The sky was cloudless and magnificent and the stars shone brighter than they do with us. We noticed that the town had been illuminated; the good inhabitants, three-quarters of them Jews, wanted to show their pleasure at seeing us. I had an excellent mattress on the sofa in the salon, though our hostess, her sister and her servant kept on visiting us one after the other, searching for a cup or a towel. We had to bolt the door so as to sleep in peace.

Sunday, October 3rd. We reached the frontier of the Russian Empire proper that evening, crossing a superb flying bridge over the River Nieman where the Emperor Napoleon had crossed in 1812. This was Kovno and a heavy barrier was raised to allow us to enter Russia, then immediately lowered behind our backs. On alighting from our carriages we found a carpet laid down on the steps and realised we were with the Russians sent to meet us. The Prince and Princess with the civil and military governors, the marshal of the local gentry and Prince Cherbatov, who had been attached to us, were waiting to sit down to table, the Princess flanked by the two governors, the Prince of Orange opposite her with Mama on his right and Prince Cherbatov on his left. I sat next to Cherbatov and thought him arrogant. I must admit I misjudged him totally.[1] The poor man was exhausted after eight days' wait for us in boring Kovno. It was a very good supper,

[1] Prince and Princess Shcherbatov became two of Cornélie's greatest friends at court, altogether admirable, loving their children, pious, charitable, on excellent terms with one another, though the Princess managed all business matters.

served with elegance. We took tea in the same room sitting round a birchwood table; birch makes very pretty furniture. When Their Highnesses had said goodnight we set out to admire the illuminations at the town hall, followed by such a crowd that we were constantly afraid of being overwhelmed, not to mention getting little presents from these very dirty people. At last we noticed we were being followed by two policemen who saw us safely home.

Monday, October 4th. We left at dawn, having always heard that once in Russia they drive like devils. We did not notice much until the third stage, although the road was strewn with traces, whips and bits of rope. Soon we passed a carriage which had been upset, which did not make me feel too confident in our drivers. They kept on uttering dreadful yells to urge their horses on and there was something strange about their strange monotonous din. When we drove up a little hill, it was so steep that a dozen peasants had to fasten ropes under our 'man of war' and push the wheels to help our eight small horses, harnessed four abreast, to get it to the top. Our manservant Frederick was on the driving seat. We drove the last stage into Shavel very fast, covering a verst in four minutes (about ten miles per hour), having travelled 140 versts that day.

The château where we were to spend the night was the headquarters for the garrison officers, and we were taken up a little spiral staircase to a vaulted chamber with some very clean beds and a locked piano, but not a single one of the articles absolutely necessary for the toilet. We were then conducted for dinner to Their Highnesses' apartments in the rooms belonging to the garrison commander, General van Sukhtelen,[2] who astonished me by addressing me in Dutch.

[2] General van Sukhtelen was the first of the innumerable cosmopolitan figures, some adventurers, others one-time refugees from the French Revolution, whom Cornélie was to encounter in Russian service and at court. He was wounded at Austerlitz at the age of seventeen and is mentioned in *War and Peace*. The Emperor Alexander was often accused of having a positive preference for foreigners over Russians.

He and his father were both Dutchmen in the Russian service.

The regimental band played during dinner. It was quite good and played several tunes from *Freischütz* and *Othello*, as well as a waltz from *The Barber of Seville*. The Princess wished to compliment the general and told him that she remembered the waltz some time ago in St Petersburg. He too professes to be a connoisseur of music and said it came from Vienna. After dinner we returned to our apartments, where, thanks to Pauline's servant, we managed to obtain the articles we needed, though they had quite lately – possibly the day before – been used for very different purposes. Mama's bed had fleas and Pauline's bugs, though she had had her bed remade.

Thursday, October 5th. We went a very good pace that day and soon left Lithuania for Courland which is not so poor a province; you notice this at once from the way in which the houses are built and above all from the windows which are quite big, whereas in Lithuania they are tiny holes you can hardly get your head through. After Mitau we passed some elegant country houses and though the road was sandy that did not prevent our postilions from going a good gallop, singing as they went. The pines are splendid hereabouts. They drove so fast that day that we reached Riga before their Highnesses. We stayed in the Governor-General's palace, a castle with towers and an interior courtyard. Our host, another of the Emperor's foreign protégés, was the Marchese Paolucci, an Italian by birth, the governor of the province and a general ADC to the Emperor.[3] Our apartment was the Marchese's own and consisted of several fine rooms, furnished with the greatest elegance and provided with everything we had lacked during the past few days.

[3] The Marchese Paolucci was married within a few months to his second wife, the daughter of the English General Cobley, who had lately retired from the Russian service to farm, very successfully, in the Crimea. Paolucci founded a family that survived in Russia until the Revolution. He is mentioned in *War and Peace* (vol. 3, part 1, ch. 9 and part 2, ch. 1), where he is shown as close to the Emperor and pressing for the supreme command.

We had an excellent dinner to restore our strength, preceded by glasses of liqueurs with plates of cold meat, salted herrings and anchovies to stimulate the appetite. The Marchese sat between the Princess and Pauline and did his utmost to be agreeable. He asked Pauline what she had done with her husband, then, as this made her laugh, added without waiting for an answer, 'You are divorced, perhaps?' He kept up the same tone and nearly made her choke with laughter during dinner. As soon as the Princess had retired the Marchese conducted us to our door, on the way showing us a very striking parrot of which he was very fond.

Wednesday, October 6th. So far the Russian driving had been fast if sometimes frightening. This was to be by far the worst twenty-four hour trial of the entire trip, far worse than anything in Prussia. We set out at four in total darkness and during the second stage we got into such deep sand that our eight horses, harnessed four abreast, could not pull us out. After much useless hauling we had to send a postilion back for four more horses, or rather cats, since the poor little beasts only know how to gallop on the level and are not strong enough to shift a berline as heavy as ours. This delay lost us so much time that their Highnesses, preceded by Prince Cherbatov, soon passed us driving at full tilt. Their carriage was lightly loaded and driven by a Russian court coachman who had driven them at the time of their marriage. He had been sent to meet them and kept up a gallop through the deepest sand. He was a great strong man with a long black beard and spared neither postilions nor horses. The fact was that at Kovno Their Highnesses had decided to drive to Gatchina in six days instead of twelve, as had first been arranged. This meant doubling the daily distance we had to travel.

We had only got half way to our stopping place called Gulben when dusk began to fall. We only had a little bread and cold meat in the carriage and shared it with our servant Frederick; that was all we had to eat in twenty-four hours. Finally, long after midnight, in the midst of the forest and the most appalling sand, our postilions demanded schnapps. We refused, saying 'Pashol', the only Russian word I had learnt, which means 'Go on'. So they left us and went into a little ale-house near the road. As they had not come back after some time, Frederick went to fetch them and they came back and remounted without further trouble. We did not move any faster however, and half asleep, half weeping, we consoled ourselves with Fabrice's song in *Azémia* – 'Oh how I perish from impatience to see you again, my darling land'.[4] Just to vary our pleasure, two of our horses then fell and nearly brought the carriage down with them. We got out as fast as we could and, while they were struggling to lift the poor beasts which lay as motionless as tree stumps, we brooded over our sad fate. At last the horses got up and we reached our longed for meeting place at four o'clock in the morning.

Thursday, October 7th. They were getting ready for Their Highnesses to leave though no one else had arrived; the maids and gentlemen were even later than us. After twenty-four hours of hunger and fatigue we had at least expected something hot to eat. Instead we found nothing but the remains of yesterday's supper, very prettily arranged on the table in the correct dishes but everything was cold as ice – beef with red cabbage, a partridge ragout and several other dishes, all uneatable. This put the lid on Pauline's bad temper. She was already feeling ill and began to scold as hard as could be. As for myself, I was too tired to make a fuss and made do with a cup of coffee and some bread. Mama took the whole thing in her stride and ate as I did, and so did our gentlemen who arrived soon after in a much worse state than ourselves. Their long legs had caused them dreadful discomfort in their carriage. M. de Bavay went straight to the Prince's room to ask leave to drive on next day in a country cart; they are just little hay carts but one can at least stretch oneself out full length.

---

[4] From Dalayrac's *Azémia, ou Le nouveau Robinson*, first performed at Fontainebleau in 1786 and immensely popular all over Europe for its melodies. George Sand's mother used to sing this aria with Grétry.

When we had finished breakfast the Prince appeared but did nothing but laugh at our misfortunes. When he had gone we agreed among ourselves to stop at the first good stopping place, which was Dorpat. It was a long time since I felt so tired; my back and kidneys hurt and I was only able to keep going thanks to some chocolate Pauline had and some madeira. The road was quite good, but the country dull and desolate. We reached Dorpat about four o'clock and were taken to a merchant's house with fairly clean rooms. M. de Bavay came to dine with us; he had a temperature and a great deal of pain in his legs.

Friday, October 8th. We had hardly lost sight of Dorpat when our postilions began to shout at the tops of their voices. We asked the reason and our servant pointed out a wolf about two hundred paces away, running along quite close to some people who were working in the fields. He was very dark and the size of a very large dog. In this connection our servants told us a story they had heard at Dorpat. It was said to have happened about fifteen days before but it seemed hard to believe. A peasant was riding home from Dorpat market mounted on a rather wretched horse he had just bought. He was probably drunk and fell asleep as he rode. In this condition he met a wolf who attacked his horse and devoured the poor brute without doing any harm to the man, who was left lying astride his horse's remains and slept there until the following morning.

We stopped to eat a meagre dinner on Lake Peipus, where the posting inn at Nenhall is spacious but like all inns on this road has no beds, only hard leather sofas. Lake Peipus is enormous with gigantic rocks scattered along the shore as though they had fallen from heaven.[5] There was no question of a bed until we reached Gatchina, so we drove on all night by quite a good road. Two of our gentlemen, driving in a peasant's cart,

[5] According to the ancient legends in the neighbourhood this is what had happened, as is recounted in the Finnish epic *Kalevala* and in the music of Sibelius – myths of which early nineteenth-century travellers could have known nothing.

had a little adventure which made the story of the peasant asleep astride his horse's carcase seem less unbelievable. Their driver saw something lying across the road and got down to remove the obstacle. It was a man fast asleep. They shook him and beat him and flung him about as hard as they could, but he could not be woken; he was dead drunk. Finally the driver dragged him away face downwards in the mud. He showed no signs of life except to give a little groan, so they threw him down by the ditch and the gentlemen drove on.

At every relay we found our drivers sleeping around a bivouac fire with the horses tethered. The postmasters woke them up with whips and they had their revenge by knocking the horses about, while the wretched animals, exhausted by fatigue, let themselves be guided by a little piece of string without a bit or proper headstall. I cannot describe how melancholy I felt the first time I saw a peasant patiently accept a blow from a postmaster's switch without seeming to mind any more than an ordinary man would mind a word of reproach. His heavy sheepskin was bound to lessen the force of the blow but it did not seem any less of an outrage to me. At one of the posting stations I heard the peasants singing a melancholy song. At the same time they are always shouting like madmen and this seems to act as a great stimulus both to them and to their horses.

Saturday, October 9th. At seven in the morning we reached Narva in time for breakfast and a visit to the famous Narva Falls, a superb cataract which is a magnificent sight. About four we wanted to stop for a little meal but a sort of quartermaster informed us in bad French that supper was waiting for us at Koskovo, two stages further on. So we got back into our carriages, which were surrounded by a group of peasants, all standing respectfully hat in hand. As it was raining I signed to them to put their hats on; they bowed deeply and explained to one another what my signs meant, but only one of them put his hat on his head, taking six steps backwards as he did so. We found a good supper at Koskovo but the quartermaster then

[36]

asked us to wait another two or three hours so as not to arrive at Gatchina in the middle of the night. We had to agree and tried to rest a little on the usual big leather sofas, hard as stone, on which we lay down fully dressed. It was midnight when our carriages were ready. The road was swampy and our horses hardly able to move. At half past five in the morning of Sunday, October 10th, we reached the end of our journey and drove into the first courtyard at Gatchina.[6]

Late October: Gatchina

Sunday, October 10th. After breakfasting we hastened to go to bed so as to get a little rest. The daylight prevented me from sleeping, though after an hour I had begun to doze a little when I was woken with the agreeable news that we must hurry to get dressed with trains and diamonds so that we could be presented to the Dowager Empress Maria Fedorovna as she came away from the church service. Mama had been summoned to the Princess's presence before dressing and had seen the Empress who had been against our dressing up in our best. When Their Highnesses had said it was her due, she replied 'I am not Empress here; I am Madame de Gatchina.' However our Highnesses insisted and we had to obey. So about eleven o'clock we went to the Great Hall where the court met before and after the service for the Empress to receive presentations. This is what she was doing when we came in and took up our positions near the door like three scabby sheep, facing the court which was really quite imposing for a débutante like me. After a short while the Empress came up to us.

[6] The palace at Gatchina was built by Catherine the Great in 1766-81, to designs by Antonio Rinaldi, for her lover Prince G. G. Orlov. The original two-storey open galleries were altered by Paul after Orlov's death. Paul and his wife Maria Fedorovna had the interior, left unfinished by Cameron, redecorated by Vincenzo Brenna, and they made this and Pavlovsk their main residences. Gatchina was burned and gutted by the German army during the Second World War and has since been restored.

She is a tall woman, quite stout enough for her height and very well preserved for her sixty-five years, thanks to a thousand little devices of dress. Her corset is so tight that she can only take very short steps and cannot even bend or put out her arms far enough to pull on her gloves when she is wearing long ones; she manages by putting her hand behind her back. She has a great deal of dignity combined with affability of manner. The Princess presented us; Pauline already knew her. She greeted us in the most cordial manner, after which she gave her arm to her daughter and left the Hall, nodding a farewell salutation to the court. She wore a cambric or muslin dress, a very pretty yellow checked shawl which I took for cashmere but which was only English, and a plumed hat.

As soon as she left the room, the court moved towards us, and M. d'Albedyll, the Court Marshal who already knew Pauline, presented us. Among all the names he mentioned I caught that of Mlle Kochetov, of whom Countess Fritsch had spoken at Weimar, saying she was very amiable and polite. I spoke to her of this introduction and she always showed us a great deal of friendliness. Her only fault was that she seemed too fond of laughing for a woman of thirty. She is maid of honour to both the Empresses since the courts are not divided; the Dowager Empress always has several maids of honour in the country. The Grand Duchess Elena's court is also lodged at Gatchina. Princess Gagarin, whose husband is the Dowager Empress's Chamberlain and a sort of factotum, and old Countess [later Princess] Lieven, whom I ought to have named first, completed this numerous company. I only mastered their names later on. They all showed us a great deal of politeness and so as not to be behindhand on our part we at once paid our respects to old Countess Lieven, a *dame à portrait* to the Empress and her particular favourite; she had superintended the education of all the Grand Duchesses and her advanced age dispenses her from much ceremonial and etiquette. Among other things she never attends a Russian liturgy [being a Lutheran]. I had felt a little afraid of her but was soon disarmed by her tone of frank good nature without brusqueness. All the court ladies come to see her almost every day and the younger ones treat her with the respect due to their mothers.

When we left her we took off our trains and put on simpler dresses so as to go on with our visits round the enormous palace (very tiring to the legs), calling on Princess Gagarin and all the maids of honour in their lodgings off the dirtiest and most stinking corridors I ever encountered in my life. No daylight or fresh air reaches them. These ladies' rooms are small and low and so heated that you risk a fainting fit in them. Most of them were not at home to us; they were busy dressing. In the underground part of the palace we came upon some guard rooms where the smell was so disgusting that you could not pass through them without holding your nose. These visits were all the more tiring because we were quite unable to understand the servant we had been allotted, as he could not speak a word of anything but Russian.

We only had a moment's rest before dinner, which is at three o'clock. Pauline and I went to the Arsenal, a large vaulted hall which was once a stable and is now used as a drawing room and as a dining room. It is divided in two by a partition with a doorless archway in the middle. One half contains a dining table and afterwards, when it has been removed, the sideboards and a swing; the other half all kinds of games. There is a little theatre, a piano, a card table, a wooden chute, a billiard table, a cup-and-ball set, shuttlecocks, racquets, dice-boxes etc. etc. The Empress's presence does not interfere with all these games, in fact she encourages them and sometimes plays shuttlecock herself.

Today the Grand Marshal, M. d'Albedyll, did the honours and we renewed our acquaintance with the ladies we had met in the morning and sat down to table. After the soup we were offered little pies of different kinds served on a single dish; then some cold chicken with smoked tongue and veal and some other things in aspic flavoured with Rhine wine; then some tasteless, flavourless beef garnished with inferior potatoes, cabbages, turnips and carrots, all on the same dish; then some fish, one or two truffle ragouts and a roast usually consisting of chickens and pullets, followed by a cream and then a jelly, red and yellow on alternate days. That is the menu at the Empress's table from January 1st to December 31st. The cooks themselves, in red liveries, serve the dishes. For dessert they served us water melons, pink inside with black pips – very nasty to taste though the Russians like them very much. The grapes (from Astrakhan) are excellent. There were also very good bergamots and masses of sweets. The company ate these all through dinner and sent loads back to their rooms. Ices are served every day – five or six different kinds on the same dish. All the ladies sit on the same side of the table with the gentlemen opposite. When dinner is finished the young court ladies began to slide down the chutes, standing up, with a great deal of grace.

Monday, October 11th. There were more worries about dress. The reigning Empress had come to see the Princess and we had to be presented. We were advised to be ready in long dresses at half past ten. Soon afterwards we proceeded to the Princess's drawing room with our gentlemen. The Empress was in the Princess's closet and we had to wait till two o'clock before being admitted to the Sanctuary. She was wearing a very simple silk habit and a small hat. Her complexion is horribly bad and she shows few signs of the beauty that was once so much admired. She has an agreeable voice but has let her figure go and her whole appearance is marked by the sorrows she has had to endure. Though nowadays the Emperor tries to make up for the wrongs he has done her and is very much attached to her, it is hard to heal the wounds she has received.

We changed hurriedly into dresses without trains for dinner and accompanied the Princess to the Dowager Empress's rooms, and then went to the Arsenal where we were presented to the Grand Duchess Elena Pavlovna. She is very handsome – tall and well-built with blonde hair and a beautiful complexion. One would think her more than seventeen years old, though she only reached that age a few months ago. Pauline introduced me to General Chernyshev;[1] he is one of the Emperor's general ADCs and is attached to the Prince of Orange to whom he is devoted. He had already been to Brussels where Pauline had made his acquaintance. He told me that he thought he had some right to my good opinion since it was he who had first thought of the marriage of the Grand Duchess Anna Pavlovna to the Prince of Orange, and so suggested it to the Emperor. This remark was not made without vanity and gave me a notion of what the man was like. As I got to know him better my opinion of him was confirmed. He is tall and well-built, but unfortunately well on in years [he was thirty-nine] and anxious to hide the fact from everyone. He thinks all the women are mad about him and only talks of himself and his great deeds. He has been married twice; he was divorced from the first and lost the second a year ago. He pretends to regret her infinitely but you would not think so when he is with women who attract him. He is so much swayed by vanity that he is frequently unbearable.

Tuesday, October 12th. I at last had a quiet breakfast with Mama without having to bother to dress. It was fine but cold and we decided to have our stoves lit, which we had refused to allow at first. We took a walk in the palace garden with Pauline. It is very pretty but very low and swampy in some places; there are some attractive summer houses, a very small orangery, some stone and wooden bridges, some little ferry boats to cross the water channels and as a rule a pensioner to ferry one across. The garden is looked after by pensioners; they sweep the paths after snow and sand them when they are slippery. We are told however that this is nothing compared with the care taken over the gardens at Tsarskoe Selo, the palace occupied by the Emperor and Empress. A horse cannot pass there without its traces being cleared away at once.

[1] Alexander Ivanovich Chernyshev (1785-1857), a favourite with both Emperor Alexander I and Nicholas I, was rightly famous for his intelligence work in France in 1807-12, where he was favoured by Napoleon and flirted with his sisters. He became Minister of War from 1826 until 1852, and was created Prince in 1853. He married for the third time in 1829.

The Imperial family dined in the Arsenal and as I went there directly with Pauline without attending on the Princess I had time to observe the effect produced by the entry of the Dowager Empress. A moment beforehand the messengers [*skorokhody*, invariably negroes] in their black plumed head-dresses go bustling backwards and forwards, then a foot-man comes in carrying a red-hot shovel of scent. The court take their places murmuring 'They are scenting the rooms; the Empress is coming.' The men stand on one side, the women on the other. At last you hear the word 'Hush' and a whispered 'Hush' goes round the hall. A little door opens, the goddess appears and everyone bows or curtseys very low. After a few words with almost everyone the Empress sits down and people take their places. I had soon established mine between Princess Khilkov and Princess Volkonskii, two of the young maids of honour, who were very friendly to me. Princess Khilkov taught me a few words of Russian and they were often very useful with the servants.

The Princess goes through our rooms every morning on her way to call on Countess Lieven, who lives at the end of our corridor. It is a great honour but not much of a pleasure to be used as a passage in this way. The Dowager Empress appeared on the 14th; she was doing a very fine design of tapestry work on a frame. Later we saw some altar cloths she had worked which she sent to the Princess to look at. To finish all this work as quickly as she says, she must work very fast indeed. Unkind people say she does not do anything worthwhile and that her maids undo all her work during the night and resew it as it ought to look.

Friday, October 15th. In the evening we played guessing games in the Arsenal. Someone had to announce a syllable and everyone else had to add two or more to make a word, which someone else then had to guess. I added the word 'mission' to the syllable 'sub' and announced that by adding employment to the first syllable I made a 'virtue'. This was applauded by all and I realised what a virtue 'submission' is in Russia.

Saturday, October 16th. It had been fixed in advance for the Princess of Orange to receive people coming to pay court to her. Having put on round dresses without trains we went to the Princess's at a quarter past two. We found Countess Musin-Pushkin already in the antechamber. She is an ugly old person, a lady-in-waiting to the Empress. Countess Litta, the Mistress of the Robes, soon arrived as well. She was to make the presentations – an aged woman too, but with a pleasant appearance. All these women whom etiquette obliges one to embrace are so plastered with powder that one can only kiss them on the chin if one is to avoid a mark. Countess Litta and her husband, the Grand Chamberlain, are Croesuses of wealth.[2] They have a granddaughter, Countess Julia Pahlen, also immensely rich, who is going to unite her fortune with that of Count Samoilov, a young man of rather pleasing appearance. We had all these people to dinner. I was seated one place away from Countess Pahlen, who was wearing a sea-green cashmere shawl, a magnificent present from her fiancé which had cost 20,000 roubles. She had two bracelets on her arms, one with a portrait of Count Samoilov done as an antique bust, the other very simple with a little lock to which her fiancé keeps the key. He had not accompanied his betrothed to Gatchina but the Empress had told her to make him come the next day. The result was that she wrote him a three-page note in pencil on her knee while dinner was in progress and could not rest until they had brought her sealing wax to seal it and ink to write the address. Countess Pahlen's face is quite pretty and she has fine brown eyes, but there is something languid about her which is irritating.

Among the people who had come from St Petersburg was the author Karamzin. He is now writing a history of Russia

[2] Count Julio Pompeevich Litta (1763-1839) was an unusual type of émigré from Milan. A former Knight of Malta, he had been allowed to marry one of Potemkin's nieces, Catherine Engelhardt (1761-1829), the widow of Count Paul Skavronskii (1751-93), who had been a nephew of the Empress Catherine I. Potemkin had made huge settlements on all his nieces and the Skavronskiis had been very well provided for; hence the enormous wealth of the Littas.

which, they say, will be very interesting. It will end with Peter the Great because he says the remainder is too recent to make frank treatment possible. When he dines at the Empress's table he is always very talkative though his pronunciation of French is most unpleasing.

The French actors had been brought from St Petersburg to amuse us in the evening and so at seven o'clock everyone went to the theatre to await the arrival of the Imperial family. It is rather a pretty theatre though small. Their Highnesses sit next to the orchestra and the rest of the society audience behind them. There are four boxes, one of which is occupied by the Grand Duke Nicholas's children and another by Countess El'mpt's. There is a sort of gallery for the waiting women and servants. I found the music very sad that day, all the more so because they played extracts from *Othello* and *The Barber of Seville* in the intervals, which reminded me of home and made me wish I were there. The French company from St Petersburg is very mediocre. They acted *Une journée à Versailles, ou Le discret malgré lui* [3] and *Le précepteur dans l'embarras*. [4] After the performance we went back to the Arsenal for supper served at round tables for twelve or fifteen people each. The Empress did not sit down but went round all the tables chatting with everyone and often forcing people to remain seated while she talked to them. She seemed to pay particular attention to a general ADC called Oom. [5] This man talks very pleasantly and is very polite but it gave me a strange feeling when I heard his name.

Sunday, October 17th. We all accompanied the Princess to the Russian service, so as to please the Dowager Empress who likes one to go when there is no other church to attend. In the country you can go in muslin or a high silk dress wearing a hat or bonnet. The chapel is in the right wing of

[3] First performed at the Paris Odéon on 20 December 1814.
[4] First performed at the Comédie-Vaudeville-Ambigu on 23 July 1823.
[5] 'Oom' in Dutch means 'uncle'. A family of that name existed in Russia until the Revolution.

the palace, and serves as a passage for everyone on their way there from the main palace block. You try to lean against the wall as much as possible because you dare not sit in a Greek church. Their Highnesses who are pregnant or feel ill sometimes allow themselves a chair. Though this was not the most suitable moment, I could not help staring with amazement at the thin waists of the officers of the Empress's regiment who stood against a window and looked so transparent that you could have cut them in half like wasps. All Russian officers are so terribly tight-laced that they can hardly sit down. Apart from the shell jacket and the belt which had to be pulled tight by two men, so I was told by an officer himself, they wear skin-tight breeches down to their high boots, which makes it impossible for them to bend their knees. Not only officers but ordinary troopers are tight-laced in this way, which inevitably causes aneurisms or other complaints. The Imperial family is no exception. From early youth the cadets are laced like this in the various schools, which makes their chests stick out as though they were stuffed. This unnatural state of things makes them die before their time and it is very rare for a Russian soldier to finish his period of service, supposed to last twenty-five years irrespective of the age at which he enrolled.

After the service we all went home. It was snowing so there was no walk. The Princess was to receive more people before dinner and she advised us to dress our best and above all to wear diamonds; it is the only thing that makes an impression here, because most people have so many and even the young girls are covered with them. Not one of the dresses was particularly tasteful or elegant. Countess Litta presented everyone as she had done the day before. There were more people and the party at dinner was very large. Count Samoilov, Countess Pahlen's fiancé was there; he is a fine young man but wears spectacles. Unfortunately his future bride seems much more in love than he. In the evening the Dowager Empress appeared at the Arsenal and herself began to read aloud Walter Scott's new novel *Redgauntlet*.[6] When she was tired she handed the book to General Chernyshev. The reading was only half audible to many of the company. On the following evenings it was continued by Prince Gagarin, who bellowed it out at the top of his voice, and by M. Villamov, the Empress's secretary.

Wednesday, October 20th. The Princess gave each of us a present of a very pretty bracelet.[7]

Thursday, October 21st. The reigning Empress came to dine at Gatchina with Mlle Valuev, her maid of honour.[8] She wore a very plain silk dress with a high neck and a little hat. The Dowager Empress on the other hand is more and more elaborately dressed every day, in silk dresses of the prettiest colours, with very complicated trimmings and little bonnets or most elegant hats. This time, however, she wore what was I think the oldest and least attractive gown she had. After dinner we were told that the Imperial family was not coming to the Arsenal and so we decided to take a little rest and, once back in our rooms, changed into morning costumes [redingotes]. While we were taking tea the Russian servant came in and told us a long story about the Empress and the Princess. We told him that would do, but this did not suit him at all and he returned three times more always with the same story. We did not move because we did not know where we were supposed to go. At last poor Ivan ran off in despair to fetch a valet who could speak French, and who explained that we were being asked for to go as soon as possible to the Princess of Orange, because the Empress was spending the evening there with part of the court, and that they were waiting for us to begin the reading. We were not very pleased at having to dress again and appear upstairs, and Mama asked them to be good enough in future to send us messages in a language we could understand.

[6] Just published and immediately translated into French.

[7] She refers to this in a letter to her cousins: 'cornelians and turquoises as talismans for Mama and Pauline, and for me forget-me-nots with a topaz, amethyst and sapphire clasp'.

[8] 'That brought the diamonds out again,' she wrote in a letter home. 'Long live cotton dresses and plain tortoiseshell combs.'

Friday, October 22nd. This evening was given up to the Dowager Empress's entertainment for the Princess of Orange, in which the maids of honour, full of talent, mostly educated at her Institutes in St Petersburg and Moscow, took the leading parts. The programme began with a very well acted little play called *Two Words, or The Brigands in the Forest*.[9] This was followed by a charming tableau which had been composed by the Princess before her marriage. It shows Merope on her knees before Polyphontes begging for mercy for her son Aepytus; the whole effect was delightful. Then came a ballad in action called *The Pilgrim Woman* with Princess Khilkov, who sings rather well, in the title role and M. Vsevolozhskii[10] as the troubadour. A Spanish tableau including almost everyone came next; it was punctuated by singing in which Princess Gagarin's beautiful voice could be heard. Then another very pretty ballad in action called *Isaure*, the story of a jealous lover, his mistress and her favourite dog, the innocent object of the lover's jealousy. And finally there was a Russian tableau in national costume which is really very beautiful when well presented. The men had fine black beards, and wore kaftans with flattish broad-brimmed hats. The women were in sarafans, open in front with gold or silver frogs and wide muslin sleeves. They wore wide flared head-dresses made of velvet over cardboard bases and embroidered with pearls or tinsel. The women had their hair smooth and parted in front; the young women had it plaited. Thee dresses mostly come from Moscow and the central provinces, whereas in St Petersburg you do not see them except on a few nurses. St Petersburg and its environs are inhabited by very ugly Finns.

We admired the Russian tableau in which the characters did not move at first. It represented, I believe, a Russian peasant wedding with some of the men holding a sort of guitar

---

[9] Cornélie's letter to her cousin Agatha gives a full description of this childish melodrama of heroic rescues from bandits, ending with the inevitable happy marriage. It adds a full account of every item in this amateur programme.

[10] A leading amateur who owned his own theatrical company.

[balalaika], which is the favourite Russian instrument. Then four women rose to their feet and one of them, Princess Khovanskii, sang some verses addressed to the Princess of Orange by M. Zhukovskii, a poet known for several charming poems in Russian. The Dowager Empress thinks very highly of him and often asks him to stay. These verses were sung to a national air which had been composed for the Emperor's return from the war in 1814. Every verse ends with a 'hurrah' sung in chorus and is very tuneful but rather melancholy; this seems a characteristic of this country's songs. After the singing they danced a Russian dance. There were four ladies with their gentlemen led by M. Vsevolozhskii, who performed the prettiest pantomime possible while dancing all the time. As for the women, they struck graceful attitudes rather than danced; each of them looked as if she were leading her dancer on to see if he could do better than the rest. Russian peasants usually sing in accompaniment to their dances, so the Imperial Chapel singers were placed in the wings and kept on repeating a monotonous sixteen-bar air. The audience applauded with enthusiasm. The Dowager Empress showed her court how pleased she was and the Princess thanked all these ladies for celebrating her return so prettily.

Monday, October 25th. As today was the Empress's birthday we were told we must dress our best for dinner. I spent the morning arranging my hair with diamonds and even refused to go for a walk with Princess Khilkov so as to do it better. Suddenly the Princess asked us not to wear diamonds for dinner but later, as it would be then that the Empress would be receiving congratulations. We had to obey and were the only ones without diamonds, as everyone was dressed up; the ceremony of congratulation or *baise-main* took place immediately after dinner.

Tuesday, October 26th. Trains were forbidden. So we put on fairly elegant round dresses to attend the service. Most of the ladies, myself included, had already had our hair done for the day. We dressed up even more for dinner and in the evening there was a little ball for those staying in the palace and the officers of the Empress's regiment. It lasted until fairly late, having begun with several polonaises and ended with a supper, after which I went to bed very tired. I think everyone else was too, for from then till Saturday October 30th we lived very quietly and our way of life was very monotonous. So as to vary our diversions I went for two or three rides with Princess Khilkov in a droshky. These small two-horse carriages are very low and one gets covered with mud and snow from all sides. We drove through the park outside the garden; it is simply a pine and birch wood growing on very marshy ground. There are a good many wolves, which this autumn had eaten twenty horses and four cows in the villages around Gatchina. There is also a kind of lynx; one of them was caught during our stay at Gatchina. He had the head of a cat and was the size of a large dog. Princess Khilkov also took me one morning to breakfast at the farm. It is a fairly big building with several rooms. The Dowager Empress keeps cows there, very carefully looked after. They are in a well-protected cow house on a wooden floor but the lack of pasture and the harsh climate makes it very difficult to rear them. They are looked after by Germans or Livonians and the dairy is very clean. The surrounding countryside of Gatchina is very low and marshy and I think it was to win a little land that they dug those melancholy lakes.

Mlle Kochetov took us one day to see the late Emperor Paul's apartments. There are two exactly similar rooms, one above the other, with a very charming little study in one of the towers at the back of the palace. The view is very attractive. The ground floor has been kept exactly as the Emperor left it. His books and papers are strewn about in the study and there is even the grain with which he used to feed the pigeons. There is also the desk given to him by Mlle Nelidov [his mistress]. In a neighbouring room behind a screen is the bed on which the Emperor died. It is a small camp bed on which he always slept; they say there are still traces of his blood on it but I did not go close enough to see.

His boots and all the clothes he wore that day are on a chair beside the bed. The Dowager Empress, his widow, comes to pray there every evening and the bed goes with her everywhere except to St Petersburg. There is a glass door into the Empress's little garden where several square stones mark the graves of the Emperor's dogs.

Saturday, October 30th. More people came from town and the Princess received them before dinner, to which sixty-four sat down. That evening they played *Freischütz* and I thought the music so fine and profound as to be tiring and upsetting.

Sunday, October 31st. I have been meaning to start my journal but am continually busy here without doing anything but dress, eat, sleep and go for drives.

Early November

Monday, November 1st. When the Princess came through our rooms in the morning to call on Countess Lieven, Mama was not there so the Princess invited me to accompany her. On the way back she stopped at our windows to watch the cavalry drilling in the courtyard. Every morning this battalion of the Empress's regiment drills either on foot or on horse to the sound of some bad trumpeters murdering the march from *Freischütz*. Connoisseurs do not admire these troops as much as other regiments of the Imperial Guard, but their horses are superb – especially the general's, a delicious bay, who has been his mount in action.

Thursday, November 4th. The Dowager Empress went to meet the Grand Duchess Maria of Saxe-Weimar and appointed the Prince and Princess Lords of Gatchina in her absence. In order to amuse them, a little piece was performed in the Arsenal theatre. Some of the ladies sang and one of the chapel singers sang the National Anthem which had been composed in 1814 on the Emperor's return from the campaigns [against Napoleon]. Then young Mlle Nelidov danced the shawl dance which is taught in the Institutes to make the young girls graceful. Mlle Nelidov was as graceful as can be and this dance, which is in reality a succession of pleasing poses, is very well designed to show off a fine figure at its best. I could not help thinking of a *bayadère* or Indian court dancer but the whole audience was enchanted and asked for an encore. When this was over the two little children of Princess Gagarin appeared dressed as a gentleman and lady of the court of Louis XIV. They made us laugh a good deal.

Friday, November 5th. This was the day of the Grand Duchess Maria Pavlovna's arrival. The Emperor also arrived that day at Gatchina; he had returned the day before to Tsarskoe Selo after a long tour in the interior of his empire. By eleven in the morning we were ready dressed for presentation to His Majesty but this did not take place until seven in the evening, when we were presented by the Prince. The great man did not look as handsome or as young as I had expected. It was dark in the room and his uniform was not very neat. He talked to Mama of her travels with our Queen and of their escape in a fishing boat.[1] When the Prince of Orange presents Mama to the Imperial family he always calls her 'his second mother' for the care she had taken of him in his childhood. The Emperor asked Pauline for news of all the people he had known in Brussels during his stay there, said a few words about the unpleasant climate of St Petersburg and the tour he had just finished and spoke of all the beautiful places he had seen in the Ural mountains. He is very deaf, which makes conversation with him rather difficult, but he talks very easily and has a very agreeable voice. Later on in St Petersburg, when we sometimes ran across him in the state rooms or the corridors, I thought him very much better looking than I did at Gatchina and he had a charming expression when he spoke. He uses so much scent that you can follow him wherever he goes. The Prince of Orange shouted extremely loudly when he was talking to the Emperor; they are on the closest terms of friendship.

[1] In 1795 from Scheveningen, when the Prince was three years old.

Saturday, November 6th. The Grand Duchess Maria of Saxe-Weimar received us charmingly and her daughters seemed delighted to have reached the goal they had been looking forward to so much. I do not think their delight lasted very long.

Sunday, November 7th. There was a Lutheran service at the palace in honour of the Saxe-Weimar princesses. I was surprised to learn for the first time that there was a small Lutheran community at Gatchina. The pastor preached a sermon from a paper held in his hand and made us sing without respite from start to finish. I was not much edified by the service as a whole, though I was delighted to attend a divine service after the Greek [Orthodox] liturgy. Their Highnesses went to dine at Tsarskoe Selo while we went for a drive with Mlle Kochetov in the direction of the Priory, a small building constructed by the Emperor Paul, who is said to have wanted to end his days there as Grand Master of the Order of Malta, a title he had assumed. He also assumed the right to decorate his wife and daughters with the Order. The Empress always wears it along with a small medallion of her husband; the Grand Duchesses wear a small cross rather unostentatiously below the Grand Ribbon of St Catherine. The Priory itself is not at all remarkable; the actors lodge there when they come to play at Gatchina.

Monday, Novemebr 8th. Their Highnesses dined together and in the evening there was a little performance at the Arsenal in honour of the Grand Duchess Maria, and the young Weimar princes made their first appearance. They were so much abashed in the midst of this novel court that they lost all poise and dignity.

Wednesday, November 10th. I had to take a little exercise by going for a drive with Mina, and I had a lot of trouble to avoid meeting Their Highnesses. The Imperial family appeared at the Arsenal for dinner. I was there with Pauline and children's games were played. They seemed too infantile for reasonable, adult people; there was a war game and other things of the same sort.

[52]

Thursday, November 11th. Mama had leeches applied to her and did not leave her room, while I dined and supped with Pauline at the Arsenal. After dinner the Dowager Empress visited Mama on her way to see Countess Lieven. She found a history of Russia on the table which is not at all kind about their sovereigns and asked the name of the book and its author.[2] Fortunately she did not go any further and contented herself with questioning Mama most minutely about her health. I was terrified lest she send her Russian doctor to her.[3] He is a good little man but it is many years since he had any ideas except the Empress's; he only sees through her eyes and she dictates his prescriptions and passes them round to everybody. There are also pills, large quantities of which she sent to Mama and Pauline for their colds. They were all put in the fire.

Monday, November 15th. Mama and I spent our time quietly getting ready for our departure which was settled for the day after tomorrow. We, and especially I, were extremely pleased to leave Gatchina and its colds. The Dowager Empress loves staying there and so do most of her ladies and maids of honour, because at least they see people there; in the city they are shut up in dark, dirty corridors, where they see absolutely no one except their relatives – if they have any.

Wednesday, November 17th. After taking leave of the Princess we went to the Arsenal where part of the company met for breakfast; then we bade one another fond farewells. The Grand Duchess Elena had already left for Tsarskoe Selo with her court; she was to go on from there to St Petersburg. It was a big move; they had to use over a thousand horses to transport us all. Everyone climbed into their carriages and we got into our 'man-of-war'. It was a splendid day. First of all we drove through the village of Gatchina, where there is a

[2] Such russophobe publications were not a rarity in the late eighteenth and early nineteenth centuries.
[3] Dr Ivan Fedorovich Ruhle was a distinguished surgeon and administrator who made no claim to be a physician or general practitioner.

foundling hospital established by the Dowager Empress as well as a school for both sexes. She has done some really amazing things in this field and it is hard to understand how she is able to manage so many institutions. I have been told that she is sometimes so short of money that she has to borrow from one of her ladies. Her activity is extraordinary, though she is helped by two secretaries and a council of six members. During her rounds of inspection, especially after the Gatchina season, she often takes a pile of papers with her in her carriage. Her Court Marshal holds the inkpot and the maid of honour hands her the papers one by one, while the Empress goes through them, signs and makes notes, with the carriage going at a great speed.

Cornélie was now approaching St Petersburg. The city was founded in 1703 by Peter the Great on land captured from the Swedes in the Great Northern War. Peter wanted a 'window on the West' and decided that this barren marshy site on the islands in the mouth of the River Neva would be the site of his new capital. The first buildings to be constructed were the fortress on Peter Island and the shipyards on the mainland opposite. To overcome the lack of stone in the region, Peter ordered everyone to bring materials to his new city and forbade any such construction elsewhere in the empire, conscripting labourers and imposing strict rules of town planning. The rich were not exempt and were dragged away from their homes to settle in the new city, which expanded to more of the islands. Vasil'evskii ostrov became the site of the state institutions.

Peter wanted to build a city like Amsterdam (calling it Sankt Pieter Burkh), and so started to recruit architects and craftsmen from abroad. Among the first was Domenico Trezzini, who designed the Summer Palace, the twelve state colleges on Vasil'evskii ostrov, and the Cathedral of SS. Peter and Paul, but his work, like that of his successors, was altered as tastes and conditions changed. He was followed by Andreas Schlüter and Georg-Johann Mattarnovi. Peter's favourite, Menshikov, built a palace on Vasil'evskii ostrov opposite the Admiralty and another at Oranienbaum outside the city.

Among the other architects were Jean-Baptiste Alexandre Le Blond, who designed Peterhof and the palace at Strel'na, Niccola Michetti, Gaetano Chiaveri, and a native Russian, Mikhail Grigor'evich Zemtsov.

Peter preferred the baroque, but in the years following his death in 1725 its popularity was superseded by the rococo, introduced by Bartolomeo Francesco Rastrelli, who was brought to Russia by the Empress Anna Ivanovna (1730-40). He was ordered to redesign the Winter Palace, and during the reign of Elizabeth (1741-62) he built the Summer Palace (demolished by Paul for his Michael Castle), the Anichkov Palace on the Nevskii Prospect by the Fontanka Canal, the Vorontsov Palace (later turned into the headquarters of the Corps of Pages), and the Stroganov Palace. He also designed the Smol'nyi Convent, the orphanage and later school, and reconstructed the Catherine Palace at Tsarskoe Selo.

Elizabeth died in 1762, to be succeeded by her nephew Peter II, whose reign lasted six months before his energetic German wife deposed him. Catherine the Great (1762-96) was a person of strong contrasts, who, unlike her predecessors, preferred to keep her public and private lives separate; and this is reflected in her buildings. Elizabeth's rococo gave way to Catherine's classicism, for which she employed such great architects as Velten, Rinaldi and Bazhenov, who were succeeded by Cameron, Quarenghi and Starov.

It was Vallin de la Mothe who designed her private residence, the Hermitage, and the Gostinnyi dvor (markets) on the Nevskii Prospect. Rinaldi built the Marble Palace, so called because it was faced with red granite and grey Siberian marble, Gatchina (radically altered by Paul), and the unfinished St Isaac's Cathedral. Bazhenov built the new Arsenal and for Catherine's son, Paul, the Kamennyi ostrov Palace and later the Michael Castle. Starov built the Bobrinskoi Palace, the Gagarin country house at Nikol'skoe, the new cathedral of the Alexander Nevskii Lavra (monastery), and also the Tauride Palace for Catherine's favourite, Potemkin, which Paul turned into stables and which was restored by Alexander I.

Cameron, a Scot, remodelled the interior of Tsarskoe Selo, built the Agate Pavilion and the Cameron Gallery, and transformed Pavlovsk *for Paul and his wife. Quarenghi designed the English Palace at Peter-hof, the Academy of Sciences and Hermitage Theatre in the city, the Alexander Palace at Tsarskoe Selo, and the new building for Smol'nyi.*

Catherine died in 1796, leaving an art collection which included half a million paintings and the buildings to house them. Her son Paul's reign lasted five years: he was deposed in 1801 and succeeded by his eldest son Alexander, who shared his grandmother Catherine's enthusiasm for building and art. For him, before he came to the throne, Cameron built the Temple of Friendship at Pavlovsk, Voronikhin designed the Kazan' Cathedral to house the wonder-working Icon of the Mother of God, and Rinaldi completed St Isaac's.

During Alexander's reign taste in architecture changed to the fashionable neo-classical Empire style. Brenna did the interiors of Gatchina and Pavlovsk (both of which were gutted during the Second World War and have since been restored to the original specifications with the help of the original plans), and the Michael Fortress. Alexander wanted St Petersburg to be the most beautiful capital in Europe.

St Petersburg

Wednesday, November 17th. In less than four hours we were in St Petersburg. As we drew near the city the road dropped steeply and you hardly noticed the approach. It was when I saw there was a granite sidewalk on both sides of the road that I realised we had arrived. At first we only saw wooden houses and enclosures, all very neatly aligned. Then suddenly, after crossing a granite bridge, we were struck by the beauty of the view, a fine canal between two granite quays and an iron balustrade, wide straight streets with broad sidewalks, and everywhere spacious low houses – a superb panorama. Of course, I could not help feeling a little sad that I was going to spent the winter here. There is something melancholy about the vastness of these wide streets and huge squares; you hardly see any passers-by and they seem lost in space. Finally we reached the great square with the Admiralty, the Winter Palace and the General Staff building with its imposing archway;[1] we could only gaze in admiration. Then we turned into the Millionaya and stopped in front of the Shepelev Palace, next to the Winter Palace.

We were conducted to a very fine apartment which had been allotted to Mama sixty-five steps above the street. It consisted of an ante-chamber, a drawing room with three large windows, and a small semi-octagonal salon, all looking onto the Palace Square. There was a bedroom at the back and a

[1] The new Admiralty, built in 1806-23 by Zakharov, retained the old layout but is decorated with numerous sculptures, reliefs and mouldings. The Winter Palace was incorporated into the scheme so that the central square became a complete architectural unit. In 1819 Rossi converted the buildings on the south side into what became known as the General Headquarters, finished in 1829 (the column was not erected until 1832).

room for the maid. A small hidden staircase of thirty-five steps took one up to Pauline's apartment, an entresol just above Mama's little salon and her bedroom. Next door they had given me three small rooms above the drawing room, which, being loftier than the rest of the apartment, made my rooms lower and put my little windows on a level with the floor. Everything was furnished with great taste and very clean. We dined in Mama's big room and were given a second footman to wait on us. After dinner General Chernyshev was sent by the Emperor to inquire if we were well-housed. Miss Mina[2] sleeps in my antechamber and I hear her chattering loudly with the other servants. I cannot get up before eight, first because it is too dark and secondly because Miss Mina cannot rise before the stove is lit and that is always very late. There is an open fireplace in the big room, the only one in our apartment; everything else is heated by enclosed stoves, which are only lit once a day and keep their heat for twenty-four hours. This makes the temperature very pleasant, and the double windows are a great help in shutting out the cold air. Only one pane, called a *wasistdas*, is opened to air the rooms. I think a good many Russians are even afraid of the little air this pane lets in and make do by airing the rooms in their own way; that is to say by scenting them several times a day. Perhaps this is to get rid of the smell of breath, which is not as a rule very sweet here, partly because of the food and the enormous number of sweets they eat, especially at court where the ladies do not merely chew them all through dinner but send plates back to their rooms. The Princess's apartment is magnificent. One of the rooms is hung with silks of Nassau blue with Orange rosettes. The Winter Palace is inhabited by some two to three thousand people.

Friday, November 19th. This was a sad and memorable day

---

[2] Miss Mina was Cornélie's maid – her use of 'Miss' is sarcastic. She was good at arranging Cornélie's hair, but her mistress wished she was a little cleaner and less negligent. The Dutch female staff sometimes treated Cornélie unceremoniously, shouting for her, for instance, when it came to packing trunks.

for the city of St Petersburg. About nine o'clock in the morning we suspected nothing. There had been a thaw the day before, the snow had disappeared and there was a lot of wind. Dr Everard[3] came to see me and told Pauline the Neva was rising fast and it was a sight worth seeing, as this only happened rarely. He advised her to take the carriage for a drive on the quays. Fortunately she did not feel like a drive and stayed with me at the window to watch the troops entering and leaving the drill hall where they have their parades in winter. The paving stones were wet with rain and there was more and more water. A little pool formed in front of the drill hall and we laughed at the trouble the officers had in getting across it.

The droshkies and waiting carriages had to move as the water kept rising and in the end we realised the river was pouring into the city. The droshkies were only able to move with extreme difficulty, and pedestrians were walking in water up to their waists. The sight became more and more frightening and soon the whole of the huge square was nothing but a lake. I was alone to watch all this as Mama and Pauline were with the Princess, I think, or somewhere else. Then, when there had been no sign of either droshkies or pedestrians for a considerable time, two coaches and four appeared. One of them luckily got into the Millionaya, the other, belonging to Count Barclay de Tolly who had just arrived at the palace and sent his carriage home, got caught on the submerged sidewalk and the horses, buffeted by the waves and up to their necks in water, had no strength left to pull. The coachman got off his seat to try to get the coach moving, lost his footing and had to cling to a nearby lamp-post. He stuck there for a few moments, looking desperate. Someone shouted to him from a window to save himself and the horses, and leave the carriage.

At last he clambered onto the pole to get back into his seat, crossed himself several times and then set about unharnessing the horses with marvellous energy and coolness. He was just in

3 The Belgian doctor of the Prince and Princess.

time, for the water was rising so fast the the horses could hardly keep their heads above it. One of them made several leaps to save itself and looked almost as if it were trying to climb onto the coachman's box, but it calmed down. The others stayed quite still and the little postilion, a child of twelve or fourteen like the majority of them in Russia, did not move from his mount and did his best to help the coachman unharness them, which was not at all easy without a knife or any other tool to undo those soaking straps. The little postilion was the first away on his horse, on whose instinct he relied, and it followed the footway very carefully. He was followed by a second horse, then a third, and they managed to reach higher ground on their own. The coachman was the last to leave, riding the fourth horse and clapping his hands together to warm them after working so long in the cold water. The carriage stayed behind bobbing on the waves with the water up to the windows.

I thought I had seen something frightful but it was nothing by comparison with what happened further down the river, especially on the low-lying islands. Pauline was going round the palace with the Princess and saw a terrible sight from the Grand Duchess Elena's windows. It was a man perched in a tree on the Admiralty boulevard signalling for help. Getting to him was difficult because of the violence of the wind, and it seems there were very few boats in the city. However they managed to save the poor wretch. About two o'clock Mlle Divov came to see Mama. I said that I would like to see the river and she suggested that I accompany her for a short time through the Hermitage. We walked through a long picture gallery to a room overlooking the quay, which was no longer visible. I had never seen the Neva itself and might easily have thought that it always ran right under the palace walls if a few half-overturned lamp-posts had not given me a rough idea of the edge of the footwalk.

The water was being forced up to Lake Ladoga instead of following its usual course; the force of the westerly wind had driven it up from the Gulf of Finland against the stream. Fragments from the bridges (all of which were constructed on boats) could be seen floating away; they had all been smashed and carried away, while there were still people on some of them. There were barges full of hay half under water and two boats from a bridge had been thrown up against the quay, where the water left them leaning on its granite balustrade, which broke under their weight. After looking at this sad sight for a time I thanked Mlle Divov and went back to our apartment. The Emperor immediately took all possible measures to help the unfortunate sufferers; General Benckendorff was ordered to the worst quarters and helped to save several lives. He was able to get back the next day.

At last, at about four o'clock, the waters began to subside and the wind to drop, but the streets were full of every sort of debris – boat-planks, wooden furniture, bits and pieces of ruined houses; they piled up in front of the drill hall. It was only with difficulty that they managed to give us dinner that day, with water in the ground floor of the palace and a rumour that some men actually drowned in the cellar. Many households had barely got bread and many people brought their horses up into their first-floor rooms. Some of the higher parts of the town were not flooded at all, for example the Liteinyi [Foundry] Street where Princess Cherbatov lives. The Prince was in the palace when the flood began and stayed to dine with us, but his wife knew nothing of the flood except by hearsay from the people who took refuge with her, begging her to feed them for that one day.

It was the the small wooden houses – of which there are a still a great many in St Petersburg – that suffered most. The Vassilevskii and Elagin Islands, and the neighbourhood of Catherinenhof on the Gulf of Finland were the worst devastated. It was above all near this last-named place that there was the worst loss of life. A village inhabited by foundry workers was entirely washed away by the floods. The foundry, which was built of stone, was the only building to survive and the wretched workmen who were shut inside saw their wives and children perish without being able to give them any help whatever. Of course the extent of the damage was much exaggerated by the foreign press and there was talk of 20,000 people being drowned, but when an accurate count was made it was found that there were about 500 in all.

The water went on sinking all the evening and by ten o'clock there was hardly any left near the palace. There has been no disaster like this for forty-eight years, the year of the Emperor's birth [1776]; and about fifty years before that the same thing had happened. It seems that Peter the Great himself had foreseen the possibility of such disasters for his new capital, because he had given orders for a boat to be kept in every house and for the fortress guns to fire when there was a warning from Kronstadt of approaching danger. The absence of trouble had caused these rules to be forgotten. It was said that the guns had been fired but no one had heard them. We went in fear and trembling lest there be a repetition of the same disaster next day but the level of the water kept falling all night.[4]

Saturday November 20th. In the morning it had entirely disappeared and I was woken by the cries of about one hundred workmen already busy clearing the square. I was surprised by their method of work: instead of using carts to move the beams and planks they did everything by hand. A boat from one of the bridges was blocking the entrance to the Millionaya and they took it completely to pieces and loaded the beams, which seemed like whole pine trees, onto the shoulders of fifty men at a time. The Emperor stopped parades for several days and let the soldiers help the citizens empty their cellars which were full of water. Everything possible was done to help the unfortunates. Many individuals took them into their houses or

[4] This was the famous flood described by Pushkin in his 'Bronze Horseman'. Cornélie's description is comparable to those in Laurence Kelly's *St Petersburg: A Traveller's Companion* (1981), pp. 138-40, and in Robert Lee's *Last Days of Alexander and First of Nicholas* (1854). No official figures of casualties were released but later reliable estimates put the total of those who perished at 2,500-3,000. Cornélie mentioned 700 in her letter of 8 January 1825 to Agatha.

distributed food among them. A beginning was made by re-establishing the bakeries and making it possible for them to start work again. Everyone contributed as much as he could from his goods or from his fortune, and the Emperor inspected everything. We saw him one day crossing the river in a boat rowed by naval cadets. He visited the foundry near which the whole village was swept away and arrived there just when the unhappy workmen were collecting the dead bodies of their families. The sight made a profound impression on him. He drives about daily in a droshky or in a little sledge with a single horse and with no suite at all. We drove outside the city to look at the canals connecting with the Gulf, all full of bits of boats, rafts, beams and other debris. Imagine the appalling notion that this mass of rubbish may still hide the bodies of human beings carried away and drowned by the floods.

December

Monday, December 6th. The birthday of the Prince of Orange was the day on which it was decided to re-introduce the Grand Duchesses to the society of St Petersburg. The Grand Duchess Maria received in her apartments, and our Princess in hers. At ten in the morning we proceeded in dresses with long trains to the Prince's presence to congratulate him. He insisted on kissing both our hands and I embraced our dear Prince with all my heart. We went on to the Princess who was wearing the Grand Cordon of St Catherine over a dress of tulle richly embroidered with gold, with two branches of sapphires and diamonds on her head. She was covered with pearls and diamonds and looked extremely well. Mama was in flaming red and gold with a bird of paradise on her turban. Pauline was in gold lamé, and I in pink and silver with all my diamonds in my hair, which had been cleverly arranged by the Princess's hairdresser.

The Princess first received the clergy, including a Roman Catholic archbishop. The Greek Orthodox clergy have a very venerable appearance, on account of their long beards and robes. In order to talk to them the Prince had to use General Chernyshev as an interpreter. After the clergy came the Council, the Ministers and the Senate. They were all presented by Prince Cherbatov, kissed the Princess's hand and the leading members of each group were embraced by the Prince. The Princess had her hand kissed at least 2,000 times that day, and whenever there was a pause she withdrew to her room and washed it in eau-de-cologne.

We admired the smart appearance of the officers while at the same time regretting their dreadfully tight-laced waists. All the uniforms are handsome but I liked the Cossacks' best. It is very simple, a blue greatcoat and wide breeches with silver epaulettes, a white scarf and no braid. There are some very handsome men among the Cossack officers, who are under Count Orlov-Denisov's command. There is always a Cossack detachment in the suburbs of St Petersburg; they do not like being shut up in the walls of a town as they are used to ranging over the plains of the Don. All their officers have to come from that region and the regiment would not tolerate any others. After all the officers had filed past there was a short respite, if a few minutes in the Princess's apartment can be so described. I would have liked a good breakfast, but all there was was a glass of barley water for Her Highness.

After the Empress's ladies-in-waiting [dames d'honneur] had been received in her room, the Princess returned to the drawing room to receive all the ladies of the court and the town, who filed past, presented by Countess Litta. The two ex-Queens or Princesses of Georgia, who have been deprived of their thrones and live here under the eye of the Government were among them. They had an interpreter and wore their national costume, being also highly rouged. I noticed a Georgian prince among the gentlemen who was wearing glasses, which looked very odd with his handsome native dress.[1] The audience came to an end with the entire diplomatic corps, first the gentlemen, and then the ladies who formed a circle.

I had done part of my dressing in the morning by artificial light for the days are already very short, and the sun had gone down long before the end of this long ceremony. At last, at half past three, we got back to our apartment to find the sorry news that the Dowager Empress wanted to see us, and that as it was the Prince's birthday she would receive us after dinner in dresses without trains. I was quite exhausted and went grumbling back to my rooms, only to meet M. Goblet transported with joy because he and M. de Bavay had just been awarded the Order of St Anne, Second Class. His delight relieved my bad temper. After this great day we returned to our ordinary routine.

Wednesday, December 8th. Mama paid some calls in the palace with Pauline and I went back to my room to write and play a little music. Later on when I wanted to go back to the drawing room, I found no more than one little candle alight. The footmen are terribly mean about lighting because they make a profit from half-used candles, and we had to scold them the whole time to get our staircase properly lit.

Saturday, December 11th. Princess Cherbatov gave us tapioca for supper. It looks like arrowroot and seems to have the same qualities.

Sunday, December 12th. The three Protestant churches in St Petersburg competed for our attendance. This Sunday we went to the German Reformed Church, which was the second one we had visited. On the two preceding Sundays we had been to the Lutheran church where M. Reinbaud, an excellent

[1] George XIII, the last King of Georgia, had surrendered his throne in 1801 and asked Russia to protect the country from the fearsome inroads of the Persians. Most of the Georgians were glad of protection, but the Dowager Queens and a handful of princes resisted this further attempt at suzerainty by Russia, and General Lazarev was actually stabbed to death by one of the ex-Queens while paying her a visit in 1803. At the time of Cornélie's stay the Russians were consolidating their hold on the Caucasus.

preacher, is the pastor. The music is fine and the church charming but as the service only begins at eleven, it ended too late for us once Sunday presentations had been restarted at court. Mr Murald, the German Reformed minister, is less of an orator than his Lutheran colleague but preaches well all the same. He usually finishes at half past eleven, which suits us better. The pastor of the Dutch Reformed Church thought we ought to go to his church and let us know through Frederick that he would be careful to finish at half past eleven too. What is one to think of such politeness? After trying them all we fixed on his church from the end of the year.

On return from church Mama went to the Princess, and I went for a walk with Pauline on the Nevskii Prospect, the winter rendezvous of the fashionable world. I did not see much of it, but noticed in all our outings the fine faces of many of the peasants, including the coachmen, whereas the women are invariably hideous. In high society it is the same; the men are much better-looking than the women. We met M. Durnov and M. Sollogub, each of whom walked a little way with us. In the evening we took tea with the Princess, and then went to be thoroughly bored at Princess Vladimir Golitsyn's.

Monday, December 13th. Mama and I went for our first drive in a sleigh and enjoyed it very much. The following day I went for a sleigh ride with Pauline who was as delighted with it as I. You fly like the wind without even noticing that you are moving. The Princess received the Queen of Imeritia,[2] who had not been able to attend the big presentation because she was ill at the time. She has very fine eyes and would still be quite good- looking if she were not so heavily painted. She has given up wearing native dress and was wearing a train with a feather toque which suited her well.

Wednesday, December 15th. It was a beautiful sunny day, a rare thing which we had not had for fifteen days, and so we

[2] Imeritia was a small landlocked Georgian principality, unique in that its last Tsar, Solomon, did not appeal to Russia for protection in 1801 but, unlike the rest of Georgia, was conquered by force of arms in 1810.

went out. There were seven degrees of frost, the air was very keen and we had to wear veils. The river was bringing down quantities of small blocks of ice.

Thursday, December 16th. There was a thaw and some rain. These changes are very frequent in St Petersburg and the thaws melt the blocks of ice in the river to more even size, which makes them freeze together more easily later on. They come down from Lake Ladoga, and without them they say the river would never freeze.[3] It was so dark that I could not see to write on my table. I had to sit on a tiny chair by the window with my writing desk on another chair in front of me. We spent the evening at Countess Gur'ev's and, as we had been invited, had to stay to supper, which meant getting to bed at half past one. That is nothing to another lady here who never gets up before four, receives from midnight and keeps her guests till four or five in the morning.[4]

Monday, December 20th. We went round the shops in the morning with Mlle Kochetov, from which I caught a cold. I dined with Princess Cherbatov all the same, but had to leave immediately after the meal, as the Princess had asked us to take tea with her. We had trouble getting away from the Cherbatov Palace as our carriage got stuck. It had been put on runners since the snow had started and refused to let itself be pulled through the carriage arch.

Saturday, December 25th. Christmas Day was celebrated by us but no one else in St Petersburg, since the Catholics and Protestants here all follow the Russian calendar.[5]

Wednesday, December 29th. Yesterday the sky and the earth were so much the same colour that you could not distinguish

---

[3] The Neva froze in the last week of December 1824 and thawed on 19 April. This was an exceptionally late but prolonged winter for St Petersburg, where it is usual for the river to freeze early in November and thaw at the end of March (Baedeker).

[4] This was Princess Evdokia Ivanovna Golitsyn, née Izmailov (1780–1850), who was known as 'Princesse Nocturne'. Her immensely rich husband left her 25,000 serfs and was sometimes referred to as the last of the Moscow *grands seigneurs*.

[5] The Julian calendar was twelve days behind the Gregorian.

between them. The Neva is a strange sight – an enormous snow plain lost in the sky, since you cannot see the houses on the opposite bank.

Thursday, December 30th. The St Petersburg climate was behaving very changeably as usual. Today we have had a superb day and I went for a walk on the quay. The sledges were coming and going on the little fir-edged tracks across the frozen Neva. Everyone here is surprised at the news of the marriage of the King of Prussia to [his mistress] Countess Harrach. I am sorry for our Queen's sake, as she was a Prussian princess.

We have not heard of the Prince's arrival in Brussels,[6] but a letter from M. Wauthier said he had passed his suite despite their five days' start and told how they had nearly perished on the Strand, that famous spit of sand joining Memel and Königberg which I had been so afraid of on our way here and which we had avoided. A violent hurricane had caught them and the sea was beating against their carriage which could not move further. M. Wauthier had got out to see what was happening and had sunk so far into the mud that he would never have got back if M. de Bavay, standing in water up to his chest, had not helped him. Their postilions went to fetch more horses and did not return for four hours.

Friday, December 31st. We wanted to end the year with a little celebration, so we got M. Vitzthum and Countess Eglofstein to sup with us along with our gentlemen. We made some punch and talked till after midnight. I had sent Frederick to buy rum and oranges. He manages very well in St Petersburg with some Hollanders who live here, and calls each morning for orders and a little chat.

[6] He had left some days before.

1825

January

Saturday, January 1st. This was not a very enjoyable day. The idea of celebrating it by ourselves made us feel so isolated among all the people around us. Besides I had counted on going to church next day to take Communion but the doctor would not allow it. I did not stir abroad until Wednesday when I went for a drive by myself. There were three degrees of frost and the cold was very piercing despite my thick furs. Opposite the English Quay I saw a square space on the Neva which had been swept clear of snow, and a solitary man was skating there.

Thursday, January 6th. This was the first day of Christmas for the Russians. The Dowager Empress, the Empress and the whole court attended service in full dress, the ladies wearing Russian costumes. We wore ours for the first time, made of tulle and gold with feathered toques and as many diamonds as possible. These grand displays without restraint or modesty make me feel like a jeweller's shop. The whole court first assembled for this occasion in the Service Hall. Only Mistresses of the Robes were then admitted to the Empress's private room where the whole Imperial family met. The ex-Queens of Georgia, those ladies-in-waiting who have been given the Empress's portrait [*dames à portrait*], maids of honour with the Empress's cipher [*demoiselles au chiffre*] and ladies from the foreign courts remained in the hall. Holders of senior court appointments [*les grandes charges*], chamberlains and gentlemen of the chamber, maids of honour with their governesses and ladies from the city had to stay in the Chevaliers Gardes Hall, where a crowd of officers of various Guards regiments lined the way for the court to pass. The Emperor led his mother by the hand, she in a purple mantle edged with ermine. The three Grand Duchesses, Elena, Maria and Anna, followed arm in arm. Then came the Grand Duke Michael and the Prince of Saxe-Weimar, followed by the ex-Queens of Georgia and finally the whole court walking pell-mell in no sort of order. The Emperor and Empress took their places up against the balustrade, the Grand Duchesses a little further back, and the ladies even further back on the right, with the men, as many of them as could squeeze in, on the left. I stood against the wall so as to have something to lean against. When the service was over they sang, or rather chanted, a thanksgiving for the victory of 1812 with everybody kneeling. This is an annual custom and the chants are very fine. There are at least fifty singers, all perfectly trained, from small children to the basses. That evening we took tea with the Princess. Mama's eyes were very bad (probably because of the glare from the snow), and Pauline had the beginning of a brain fever which ended up making her very ill indeed.

Friday, January 7th. I went to the Dutch church alone and afterwards was walking in the little Hermitage garden when I was fetched to attend the Princess, to whom I was attached that day in place of our two invalids. After giving audience to a gentleman I did not know, she decided to take a walk in the little garden and told me, as Mama could not accompany her, that I was to dine with her at the Dowager Empress's. By this accident I was thus admitted to the 'Knights of the Round Table', as the Princess called them. These are the Empress's small private dinners in her own apartment. Besides the Dowager Empress and her daughters (and sometimes Grand Duke Michael and his wife), they are attended by her Court Grand Marshal Albedyll, one of her secretaries, Prince Gagarin, and a few privileged people from St Petersburg, usually the author Karamzin, the famous General Miloradovich, whom they call the nightingale because he never stops talking, and a little councillor called

Tutolmin, who seems to be the Empress's right hand man. The Prince of Württemberg and his sons are also often admitted to these dinners. This Prince is on a very formal footing with his sister and is not much liked here, because he is said to be so arrogant. His sons are like two blocks of wood, and they say the Prince treats them very strictly. Since the death of his wife, who used to occupy our apartment in the Winter Palace, he inhabits a fine palace on the Fontanka with his sons and daughter. We went there one evening at the beginning of our stay so as to pay our respects to the Princess of Württemberg, who leads a rather gloomy life there with Madame de Bolvillers, her lady-in-waiting.

When dinner was over everyone departed and I was left in the dining room, where all the candles were extinguished ten minutes later. Finally I was told that the Princess was going to see Countess Lieven, so I followed her there, and they withdrew together into the Countess's private room. I waited in the anteroom with a young officer, the Countess's grandson, who did his best to entertain me. Various other people arrived, and when the Princess at last reappeared I followed her to the Grand Duchess Elena's, where I nearly fell asleep waiting. It was not the first time I had been there. I already had that pleasure one evening before the Prince's departure for Brussels, I cannot remember why, though each time I was able to convince myself that antechambers are not the abode of happiness.

I remained in waiting for the next few days. This generally meant a drive or walk, and trotting round the palace in the mornings with the Princess. Nothing in the world would make her visit her mother unattended, though she has only to go through her sister's apartment on the same corridor. This sometimes meant a great exchange of compliments for me with the Prince of Saxe-Weimar, because I could not accompany the Princess through her sister's rooms and had to make a long detour to rejoin her. I found the shortest route went through the Prince of Saxe-Weimar's study, and that was how we always went when he was on parade. But if, on opening his door, we unfortunately found that he was already back, he not only asked me to come in, but would beg me to wait there for the Princess while he entertained me. I suppose it is because of his extreme stupidity combined with great kindness of heart that one is less afraid of offending him than any other potentate. I would not dare to walk boldly through any other prince's study, but that good fellow Saxe-Weimar, far from taking offence, would make a thousand apologies when he could not stay to keep me company. On one occasion he gave me *The Story of Jocko the Monkey* [1] to read when he was called away to wait upon the Emperor, but at that moment General Patkul, his ADC, came in and was ordered to entertain me.

Antechambers usually meant the company of pages and footmen. The pages were quite conversable, dressed like little officers with powdered hair and boots. It was their duty to carry the Imperial ladies' shawls and wait on them at table. When they leave the Corps of Pages they become officers in the Guards. The smallest boys are only used on special occasions and look like little Cupids.

Tuesday, January 11th. The Dowager Empress was going with two of her daughters to kiss the icon of the Mother of God in the Kazan' Cathedral. That morning the Princess gave each of us a present of a sable tail. She told me I was to go with her to the church and talked of nothing but its beauties and its memories for her. Soon afterwards we drove together to the Anichkov Palace to await the Empress in the company of Grand Duke Nicholas's children. They were playing with little Frederici, the son of the governor of Pavlovsk, who is being brought up with them. I would have loved to have played with these delicious tots, if I had not been restrained by the Princess's presence. Moreover the Empress soon arrived and we set off, the Empress in one carriage with her two daughters and the young Princess Marie of Saxe-Weimar, and the Princess Augusta went with us three ladies in another. We stopped at the

[1] A successful operetta just produced in Paris.

[72]

portico which gives onto the Nevskii, which is the finest but not the main entrance of the cathedral; the altar is on the left when you go in that way. It is a superb church with huge porphyry columns and steps leading to the choir, a solid silver grille and a magnificent Glory above the iconostasis.

The Empress and her daughters at once climbed the choir steps while we waited below. She walked towards a small altar on which the icon of the Mother of God was exposed, made three deep reverences, kissed the icon and bowed to the high altar, to her daughters and to us. The Grand Duchesses followed her example one after another and rejoined us. Then we all made the tour of the church, which is decorated with captured banners, mostly taken from the French; the keys of captured cities are also on display. The floor is paved with marbles from Siberia. General Kutuzov is buried here by special favour as a signal honour. His wife, who died only last year, was not allowed to rest beside him. Over his tomb hang the battle standards of several French regiments by order of the Emperor. Two priests were at the door when the Empress left, one of them decorated with the Order of St Anne. They are often forced to stand bareheaded in the fiercest frosts, which, I think, is why they let their hair grow so extremely thick; it looks as if it had been crimped. On leaving the cathedral we were so squeezed by the enthusiastic crowd that we could hardly keep our feet.

Wednesday, January 12th. December 31st for the Russians, and like yesterday I dined with the Dowager Empress. After dinner all the ladies kissed her hand to congratulate her on the New Year, and the gentlemen did the same. When the Imperial family left I remained the only woman there, with Countess Fritsch, to wait on our Grand Duchesses. So the gentlemen set about saluting us as well, and when I saw the Countess letting her hand be kissed, I decided to do the same, though we did not do it entirely in the Russian manner, for we should have returned a kiss on the cheek or temple to each. I could not help roaring with laughter over the ceremony afterwards.

[73]

Thursday, January 13th. This is the usual day for the great Court Masquerade, the feast to which the whole population of St Petersburg is invited, but the Empress Elizabeth's health could not stand the commotion, so it was put off till later. Mama's eyes are better, but Pauline is still ill and could not come with us to court.

Tuesday, January 18th. Pauline missed the Feast of the Kings for the Russians as well as the Feast of the Blessing of the Water and its ceremonies on the Neva. This festival commemorates the Baptism of Christ in the Jordan. A few days before they had started to build a little shrine on the frozen river, open with a sort of loggia round it where it used to be the rule for the whole court to assemble in full dress whatever the weather, a terrible custom which has been relaxed. To begin with they came out on a balcony, but this year the whole Imperial family stayed behind the double windows, with the exception of the Emperor who did not appear at all, so as not to make an obvious departure from his previous habit of sitting bareheaded on horseback through the whole ceremony, which he was not well enough to do this year.[2]

At ten I went with Mama, both of us dressed in rich gowns with trains, to wait on the Princess, who immediately left to join the Dowager Empress. As I was not of high enough rank to go with them, I had to leave them on the way so as to reach the Service Hall. Prince Cherbatov was to have conducted me, but he did not turn up and I had to make this difficult journey by myself. I had to go through all four saloons, two of which are guard rooms, and the two others were already full of officers gathered to attend the service. I had literally to fight my way through the crowd, although everyone politely gave way to me. There were very few people in the Service Hall; most of the ladies were late. The Empress soon appreared with

[2] Alexander I had been severely kicked by a horse on 1 October 1823 but had insisted on keeping all his engagements, including the Blessing of the Waters in January 1824. He had become extremely ill as a result, and this was the basic cause of his increasingly bad health throughout 1824 and 1825. The official (but misleading) diagnosis of his complaint was erysipelas.

[74]

her daughters and granddaughters, the Grand Duke Michael and the Prince of Saxe-Weimar, and we went into the court chapel. The singing was superb, and after a short service the priests left, carrying the Cross and Gospels, preceded by the choir. The Imperial family followed, with all of us behind them. We crossed the White Hall and the following chambers leading to the reigning Empress's apartments, where the negroes dressed in oriental costume stand. Most of them talk French and Russian and they follow the Emperor and Empress everywhere. The Empress's rooms overlook the river and everyone made for them.

The priests and their procession had left us at the Great Staircase so as to reach the little shrine on the river. We took our places at the windows of the Marble Hall. Despite the thaw the whole Neva and the Palace Quay were crowded with people. A path was sanded for the priests and we soon saw them come out of the palace in the order in which they had left the chapel. They were followed by the standards of the regiments of the garrison in the capital, the court pages and some officers. Most of the officers refrained from exposing their bare heads and stayed indoors since the Emperor was absent. As soon as they had reached the shrine the procession entered and the standard-bearers lined up in the open loggia. The Metropolitan then descended several steps and plunged the Cross into the water through a hole in the ice, while the fortress guns fired a salute. Two silver containers full of Neva water were sent off at once to the Empresses, the standards were sprinkled with it, and the people rushed to draw some of this hallowed water as soon as the procession with the priests had left. I was assured that they used to baptise children there by total immersion, but some of them died, so the custom had to be abolished.

Wednesday, January 19th. Our Princess's birthday, so we congratulated her in the morning, wearing ordinary dresses. As she had received people the day before there was nothing more to be done until the evening when the Dowager

Empress gave a ball in her honour. Everyone praised her dancing, which was not difficult as they dance rather badly in St Petersburg and very few people know French dances, which they regard as curiosities. The commonest dance is the Russian quadrille, for which you only need to know how to waltz and walk. Then there are waltzes, which amount to a whole ball on their own account since they play the same tune for a good half hour. Each lady goes round only once or twice with the same cavalier, after which he has to make his bow and seek another partner. The mazurka is rather a pretty dance when gracefully performed; I liked seeing it danced by a little Cossack, Count Orlov-Denisov's son. The medley always plays a great part in these balls, which they begin and end with a polonaise. The Empress went round her circle twice with extreme politeness. The rest of the time she had her lorgnette in her hand and enjoyed watching her daughter and granddaughters dancing. The ball was in the Service Hall, where all the ladies sat on chairs round the walls. I did not think the dresses very smart: a lot of blue and pink, yellow and lilac, overloaded head-dresses badly done, and lots of precious stones, a few fine pearls and many false ones. Supper afterwards was in a square dining room next to the Grand Duchess Maria's apartment. I am beginning to get used to caviar and even to like it a little.

Thursday, January 20th. A ball at the Middletons', the American minister. The rooms are a little small but the Middletons are very amiable and polite. We stayed from ten until half past eleven, just long enough to dance a polonaise and watch some waltzes.

Sunday, January 23rd. Nothing remarkable happened during the course of this week. I took walks in the little garden whenever the weather allowed, either with the Princess or by myself. The garden was swept every day which meant that we avoided the two feet of snow that lay everywhere else. We mostly saw the ladies from Weimar. It was through one of them that I got to know a new arrival at the court of Russia,

Countess Tomatis, a charming person, Viennese by birth though of Italian origin. She had lost her father and her fortune, and the Grand Duchess Maria had got her a place as maid of honour to the Dowager Empress – a most unattractive position and hardly worth the sacrifice she made in leaving her country and relations to live under a sky as grim as Russia's; but what will one not do in order to make a living?

Sunday, January 30th. I went alone to church and then dressed for the Princess's audience. After she had received a few people in her drawing room, standing as usual, she retired to her boudoir to receive Prince Yusupov, who had been a contemporary of the Empress Catherine. He told us a few stories about that great sovereign and praised her self-control. One evening he had seen her get some very alarming news from Warsaw – I cannot remember on what subject. She stopped her game to read the despatches, went through them without blinking an eye, folded them, finished her game, and then withdrew to her apartment to work all night. He talked about his stay in Leiden where he had studied with some other Russian magnates, naming all his long since dead professors to the Princess, who could not possibly have known them. This Prince lives in Moscow and they say he is a regular pasha. He has a whole seraglio, some of whom go with him on his journeys. They even say that some of the Moscow magnates keep seraglios both for themselves and for their friends. Everyone agrees that the luxurious dissipation of the old capital is incredible.

Among other people presented were two ladies, one of whom is English by birth but was educated in Odessa. Her father is General Cobley, who had made a career in the Russian service and retired to breed sheep in the Crimea. She had come to spend the winter here and been introduced to General Paolucci, the governor of Livonia. He is going to marry her and carry her off to Riga. Some people come a long way to get married.

That evening the Dowager Empress had a play performed in the White Hall, where she has had a theatre set up, a quite unnecessary undertaking in my opinion as there is a charming theatre in the Hermitage. But the Dowager obstinately refuses to regard the Hermitage as part of her apartments, whatever the Emperor may say to her on the subject. Trains had to be worn for the spectacle, and Mama came as well. We sat on chairs arranged round the room which rather spoiled the view of the raised stage. The French company performed *Le secret du ménage*, a fairly enjoyable play.[3]

Monday, January 31st. We got several letters this morning and I had only read half of them when we drove off to Countess Litta's to see the trousseau of her granddaughter, Countess Pahlen, one of the richest heiresses in St Petersburg. She owns 40,000 'souls', which is how they calculate fortunes here. There were several people visiting but only maidservants to do the honours. First of all we saw the kitchen utensils, casseroles and silver chests, then in the next room a magnificent table service and the table and household linen, not very well sewn by Dutch standards, and finally the wardrobe which seemed to me superb. Everything was embroidered, down to the sheets and pillowcases and twelve dozen handkerchiefs of exquisitely embroidered Moscow work. I counted thirty-five silk dresses of different colours, eight or ten muslin, one of Brussels lace, a dozen embroidered petticoats with double flounces, splendid furs, lace pillows and counterpanes and even pink satin slippers covered in lace. I also saw a morning costume of Russian work in cashmere shawl stuff, the texture and the colour lovely and the borders natural flowers on a white ground. Finally the finest thing of all, the future husband's dressing gown and bedspread, both of genuine striped cashmere. The Russians think the trousseau mean for such a fortune, but I thought it splendid. People are spoiled here by their enormous wealth and their still more vast extravagance. I hurried home for my walk with the Princess in the little garden and regaled her with descriptions of what I had just seen. She retorted by describing all the unpleasant experiences she had had to put up

[3] First performed at the Théâtre Français in Paris on 25 May 1809.

[78]

with at the time of her own marriage, like receiving congratulations while still in bed.

February

Tuesday, February 1st. Pauline went for her first drive with me to Vasil'evskii ostrov and it was the first time I had crossed the river. As soon as the ice was strong enough they restored the carriage bridge. The Vassil'evskii ostrov quarter is much quieter than the left bank; few society people live there but there are a lot of merchants. On our way back we saw them cutting blocks of river ice, a good two and a half feet thick and four to five feet long. After I had changed I went to see Countess Tomatis. I found a Polish [Livonian] maid of honour there, Mlle Glasenapp, together with her brother, a colonel in the Polish regiment of Uhlans, who had just arrived from his garrison to see his sister. He talked a great deal in an interesting way. All the same, when I came to see more of him later on, I thought him excessively pleased with himself. That day he talked of nothing but Siberia where his father had been a governor-general. He and his sister had been to visit him and stayed for a fairly long time. Although the climate is as cold as northern Russia it is much less changeable and the air is purer. The country is rich and fertile, with mines of almost every metal and quarries of every sort of marble. The roads are good and well maintained. The crops are harvested within six weeks. The people are good and exceedingly honest. This evening's talk was like a lot of other conversations I had in Russia, which gave me a very different idea of Siberia from what one generally has in Europe. The exiles work in mines or are shut up in fortresses and you do not see them.

Wednesday, February 2nd. The Prince of Saxe-Weimar's birthday. He received the court's congratulations in the morning with his wife. The Emperor ordered a play for the Hermitage theatre that evening but did not attend himself. This has a charming amphitheatre, which leaves just sufficient room for the Imperial family's places and their suite's just behind the orchestra. I went there in advance with Mlle Kochetov. Pauline reappeared in society that evening and first went with Mama to the Princess's so as to see the Dowager Empress. All the invited ladies were placed on the right and the gentlemen on the left. Their beautiful dresses with trains made a charming affect. When everyone had taken their seats the Empress came down the steps on the Prince of Saxe-Weimar's arm to the sound of a musical fantasy, which made our ears ring, and the rest of the Imperial family followed her. They gave a short French play and then the Russian dancers treated us to an extravagant ballet. They have a passion for this sort of entertainment here, which to my taste is the most insipid thing in the world.[1]

Thursday, February 3rd. Walking with Mama on the Neva quay this morning we saw the Emperor without recognising him. He was wearing a grey greatcoat with red facings, like all officers, and was in a small sleigh drawn by a single horse. This is the modest little carriage he uses all the time. I asked Mama who this officer could be who was so civil and saluted us as if he knew us well. She did not know either, and it was only later that I learned from the Princess that it was the Emperor. She herself had encountered him that day and would not have recognised him without the help of Pauline, who was with her. She took pleasure in telling her brother this story, and some days later, when he met us in the corridor, he spoke to us about it, adding that our surprise at his politeness did not say much for his officers in general. There was a ball from eight till one o'clock in the morning and I felt very tired. They finish with a very long cotillion, after a 'tempeste', two French dances, two Russian quadrilles, a mazurka, some waltzes and three polonaises.

Saturday, February 5th. The three of us drove over to Kamennyi ostrov this morning. It is an island on the Neva

[1] Cornélie changed her mind about ballet when she saw Taglioni dance in Paris in 1834.

where the Emperor and several other people have country houses. The palace looks fine but we only caught a glimpse of it in passing with its greenhouses and gardens, which they say are very big. Everything was covered in too much snow to risk approaching. All during our drive we saw garden walls completely down and houses badly damaged. Our coachman tried another road and we drove past the Pensioners' Hospital near the palace, but our horses sank so deep in the snow that we had to turn back quickly. Our doctor, M. Everard, has decided to learn Dutch and has asked me to correct his lessons and make him read aloud.

Wednesday, February 9th. The great feasts were beginning, and it has been decided some time since to compensate us for being so long deprived of our pleasures. It was the Grand Duke Michael's birthday and a ball was given in his honour in the White Hall. Ordinarily balls in the White Hall are only given for the birthdays of the Emperor and Empress. Mlle Kochetov came to fetch us about eight to take us to the White Hall, so called because it is white stucco with white marble columns, which were hung with wreaths of lighted candles, not perhaps very prettily arranged but emphasising the brilliance of the room by their mere numbers. It looks much better than the neighbouring St George's Hall with its red walls and columns, too dark to be lit properly by all its forty-one lustres and sixteen candelabra. What is more, the marble sweated and the heat transformed this damp into a sort of mist that filled the card-room. On each side of the throne there was a buffet covered with gold plate where they served tea. The other refreshments at court balls are rather meagre, consisting of one large dish of sweets and a few glasses of lemonade. The orchestra was in the White Hall, which was kept exclusively for dancing. The dances were mostly polonaises, partly out of courtesy to the Emperor who at last made an appearance, partly because trains were compulsory in the White Hall and this made other dances difficult for the ladies, several of whom did their best to show off to advantage, mostly without success. I myself danced eight polonaises, which makes a good hour's walking, and thoroughly enjoyed myself. Dancing with the Court Marshal, Monsieur Naryshkin, I learned that such a party required about 10,000 candles, including the supper room.

Supper was in the Marble Hall, which forms part of the Emperor's apartments. Our tables were covered with hyacinths and jonquils, and we found bunches of them afterwards in our rooms. The tables all stood under orange trees whose tubs were covered so that the tree trunks rose out of the table centres. There were vases full of flowers all around. The diplomatic corps are only admitted to the biggest court functions, and the splendid malachite centrepiece had been placed on their table. The Imperial family's table was in the middle of the room, where the Grand Dukes and Duchesses sat with the Georgian ex-Queens, the Princes and the principal ladies of the court. The Emperor retired when everyone was seated, and the Empress made a tour of the tables. There was fine music by Rossini during supper. An upper gallery all round the room was filled with curious onlookers, as in the White Hall; these were all ladies, as men were not admitted. There were a few more polonaises after supper, and the Imperial family retired at half past one. There had been between 700 and 800 people at the ball, but it did not seem at all crowded because of the size of the rooms.

Thursday, February 10th. We called on Countesses Lieven and Elmpt and visited the Court Marshal's wife, Mme Naryshkin.[2] The Naryshkin family bears no title, considering itself sufficiently noble for having produced the mother of Peter the Great. Mme Naryshkin usually receives in her boudoir, adorned with pictures and all sorts of pretty pieces of furniture. Like all great Russian ladies she has a suite of impoverished dependent females sitting in her salon. One almost always finds two or three agreeable talkers there and she herself is very amiable, like her husband. That evening we talked about

[2] Née Princess Lobanov-Rostovskii, and no connection of the Emperor's former mistress.

festivals, and M. Naryshkin told us that 70,000 candles had been got ready for the Tauride Palace display. A gentleman who had just arrived from the country changed the subject by talking of the losses Russian peasants had suffered that year for lack of haulage. It was a fairly severe winter by our standards, but a mild one for Russia, and haulage on the principal roads to the capital from the south had often been interrupted by thaws, very much to the disappointment of the peasants who are accustomed to driving hundreds of versts with all sorts of provisions, including whole pigs and bullocks, game and birds of every kind. The slightest thaw spoils all this merchandise. There is the same difficulty of communication between distant provinces. Some suffer from shortages while others have so much grain that they do not know what to do with it. It is only the winter haulage that can rectify the situation, for the roads are too bad for goods to pass at any other season.

Friday, February 11th. Mlle Glasenapp had fixed an appointment for me at midday to come and see her brother's Italian drawings. Countess Tomatis came with me and I thought the whole collection would amount to a couple of albums. Instead Mlle Glasenapp sent for her brother in person and he arrived accompanied by such a quantity of portfolios of all sizes that I was almost frightened. We bravely set to work to look at them; however, it must be admitted it was worth the trouble. Besides a lot of sketches of costumes and scenes in colour, there were a number of beautiful Italian views drawn in pencil with extraordinary precision and real talent. There were some portrait sketches also, including a self-portrait. The artist had put himself into every drawing he could manage. He had even sketched a duel he had provoked by making caricatures, which left him with a big scar on his forehead. M. Glasenapp owns a couple of very precious drawings by Michelangelo and Salvator Rosa, which are very worn and can only be appreciated by connoisseurs. To vary our pleasure Mlle Glasenapp gave us breakfast while her brother sat down at the piano and sang. His musical talent did not seem at all extraordinary, though he is much admired. As a finale he showed us a huge pencil drawing made on the hills above Florence with a view of several leagues of country and the beauties of the Arno valley. After seeing that I ran away at full speed as it was after three o'clock, and Mama and Pauline could not imagine what had happened to me.

That evening we paid several calls in St Petersburg but only found Mme de Hogguer at home with a couple of Dutchmen who are living here, M. Buis and Count Heyden. M. Buis is a small, rather malicious eccentric, very popular in society, knowing all the news and criticising everything he does not like. He is an arch-republican who refused to return to his country when it became a kingdom under Louis Bonaparte. He prefers to remain in Russia where he told the Emperor himself that, now that he had lost his ancient privileges as a patrician of Amsterdam, he preferred to live under an absolute despot. Count Heyden is in the Russian service. He had been given a command in Finland, but had been accused of favouring smuggling. He is, as a result, 'under judicial inquiry', a state of affairs that can last for ever in Russia, where justice is not well administered. He has been cleared of favouring contraband, but not of negligence in doing too little to prevent it.

Sunday, February 13th. After dinner the Palace Square came to life with a huge number of sleighs full of merchants and their wives driving round and round the palace in a continuous line. They say it was in the hope the Dowager Empress would show herself at one of the windows after dinner. This happens almost every Sunday, when there are also horse races on the Neva. There is an enclosure on the river with a stand in the middle for the judges. The horses, some of which are very good trotters, are harnessed to tiny sleighs only big enough to hold the driver.

Monday, February 14th. Mlle Sylvestre fetched me to look at M. Glasenapp's drawings again. He had moved to Countess Eglofstein's with his whole show. Lebzeltern, the Austrian minister, called with his wife, who was born Princess Trubetskoi.[3] We talked and I did not get back until half past ten.

Tuesday, February 15th. The Princess's nameday. She received congratulations in the morning and we were in attendance in morning dress. Among the lesser persons coming to congratulate her was a Dutch gardener, long established here, who gave her a pretty table covered with hyacinths, lilies, tulips and snowdrops. In the evening the whole court went to the Grand Theatre (by name only as it is not at all large) to see a national play called *Pozharskii*.[4] As I did not understand a word I was rather bored. The play was followed by a ballet, *Flore et Zephyre*, in which I thought the ballerinas very indecently dressed.

Wednesday, February 16th. The day I have been dreading – the Great Masquerade postponed from New Year's night. We dined alone and at eight o'clock set out in evening dresses without trains, the plainest ones we had because we had been warned they might be torn to shreds. We went first to the Service Hall, the meeting place for all the people connected with the court. Most of the ladies were wearing Russian dress, which is most practical because it stands up best in the mêlée. The gentlemen wore little Venetian cloaks which gave them a singular appearance. The Imperial family soon appeared, with the Emperor leading his mother by the hand and with his hat on his head. All the men followed his example with their hats. A polonaise was formed at once to go to the St George's Hall by

---

[3] Lebzeltern was considered by Metternich to be his cleverest subordinate until he was implicated, through his brother-in-law, Prince Trubetskoi, in the Decembrist Uprising in 1825. Cornélie knew or met many of the diplomatic corps in St Petersburg: Canning from London; de la Ferronaye, de Lagrené and de Fontenay from France; Ludwig van Heeckeren tot Enkhuize, considered the cleverest Dutch diplomat, whose career as minister in St Petersburg from 1823 to 1837 was ruined by his involvement in Pushkin's fatal duel, and later minister in Vienna; Baron Palmstierna from Sweden; Middleton from the USA; Prince Hohenlohe from Württemberg; and Count Ludolf from Naples.

[4] This is one of various dramatic pieces based on the history of Prince Pozharskii, who in 1612 led with the butcher Minin the national rising which expelled the Poles from Moscow and restored the monarchy under the first Romanov tsar.

way of the White Hall. All the apartments on the way were already full of people, merchants and the like. The fine folk gathered in St George's Hall but everything was soon in complete confusion. The polonaises were the sole salvation because society people were alone in dancing them and so they were the sole means of safety. There is no shame in asking a gentleman to have pity on you and stay with you till you are in a safe place. I only had three or four partners the whole evening. The Dowager Empress sat at a card table on the right of the throne in St George's Hall, where I knew she would be, with several places round her for the Grand Duchesses and any ladies who could get there. But there was such a crush near the throne that, not being able to even see the Empress's table, one was happy to be carried away in a polonaise which took one into slightly fresher air. In some places, especially by the doors, the heat was almost unbearable. The crowd made way with difficulty for the polonaises to pass, and as no police were tolerated in the palace that day, it was only by saying 'Gentlemen, please let me pass' that you could get through the enormous throng.

Fortunately I was never at the head of one of the polonaises. Thus I was able to take a good look at the singular spectacle of this horde of people lined up on either side of us, Russians with long beards and faces full of character, their women in their national dress which loses all its elegance on their neglected figures, women from Kazan' in their pointed head-dresses, Greeks, Tartars, Turks and Persians in their national costumes, even Kirghiz from Asia with rounded shining faces come to give *kumiss*[5] to the reigning Empress who cannot bear it, and finally among all these a somewhat higher class, merchants dressed like us, others in hats etc., etc. There were altogether over 21,000 individuals, not counting the court, whose tickets had been taken at the door; 24,000 or 25,000 had, I believe, been issued. Mina and Maria, both our maids, came, as well as Frederick the footman who wore one of Maria's black aprons as a Venetian cloak.

[5] Fermented mares' milk.

Apart from the White and St George's Halls the polonaises traversed all the Emperor's great apartment and his very long corridor, and returned though the apartments of the Dowager Empress. There was an orchestra in every room and buffets at intervals, resplendent with gold and silver plate but behind balustrades. Refreshments were served to everyone, every sort of drink except strong spirits. Everyone asked for something so as to be able to declare that they had drunk or eaten with the Emperor. I danced through all the rooms three times, after which I was lucky enough to reach the antechamber to St George's Hall, which leads to the Hermitage. There I was able to find half a chair which someone was kind enough to let me share, and I stayed there until it was time for supper. Several society women were in Russian costume, two were noticeable for their beauty, Mesdames Tatishchev and Zavadovskii. The first is not very young and does not have a brilliant reputation, the latter is a girl of about seventeen who was married last autumn. She is like a lovely statue, quite without expression when she speaks.

We went into supper at about eleven, having obtained tickets of admission to the Hermitage, where only specially invited people were admitted. I set off a little early with M. Goblet who was my partner. The whole of the Hermitage was lit up to charming effect, and we could breathe easily while waiting for the Imperial family to pass so that we could join in their procession. Eventually we reached the theatre where the decoration was incredibly beautiful. The floor had been raised to the level of the stage so that there were only four or five steps to descend, and the effect from above was magnificent. The semi-circular backdrop was a regular design of tiny windows with little lights behind each pane and a mighty crystal lustre hung over the centre of the room.

The Emperor retired as soon as everyone was seated, but the Empress sat down and did not go round the tables. Conventional music was played during our entry but it was soon replaced by a delightful melody sounding like perfect organ music. It was in fact an orchestra of horns played by as many men as there are notes on the instrument.[6] These unfortunates are condemned to produce one single note all their lives and to do so with astonishing precision. They sometimes have to count up to two hundred before playing their mi or re. Almost all the Moscow magnates maintain such orchestras in their country houses. They say the invention was introduced into Russia by a German about fifty years ago. The combination of this music with the beauty of the room, and with the flowers that covered the tables, gave an air of fairyland to the whole picture. As I left I took one final look back from the top of the steps at what was certainly one of the loveliest sights I saw in Russia.

We then danced a polonaise back to the crowd waiting in St George's Hall and I went round the rooms once more with M. Goblet until we met the Imperial family just as they were leaving. I took advantage of this lucky chance to join Pauline and we were back in our apartments by half past midnight, leaving the crowd to enjoy the pleasure of remaining in the Imperial palace for several hours more. My costume had survived very well. My dress had not a single tear. People had greatly exaggerated the risks involved in this great party which I am delighted to have seen. My only trouble was the extreme heat which made me perspire prodigiously and put my hair so completely out of curl that it hung straight down my face.

Thursday, February 17th. We rested.

Friday, February 18th. Mlle Kochetov suggested I go with her to see the 'Russian Mountains' [slides] which had been constructed on the Peterhof road near a tavern called the 'Krasnoi kabak'. The weather was pleasant and we set out by sleigh, but it turned out that we had gone too early. The mountains were there but no one was sliding yet either at the 'Krasnoi kabak' or along the road. So we drove back to the city and visited the Champ de Mars to see the Russian people amusing themselves during the last week of carnival. They were sliding

[6] Horn orchestras were introduced into Russia about 1770 by a German impresario.

down ice mountains there. Ordinarily these are built on the Neva but, though the ice was more than three feet thick, it was not thought strong enough, especially in view of the changeable weather. Besides the mountains there were roundabouts and booths with Pulcinellos showing off their tricks to clanging music. There were not many people yet, but when Pauline and I went back in the evening we found two lines of carriages driving round the square.

Sunday, February 20th. After going to church with Mama we three took a walk along the quays and the Fontanka, which they call the Emperor's walk. Since all the Imperial family uses it care is taken to sand the sidewalks better than elsewhere, which is why we also used it for our daily walk. The only tiresome thing is to be always followed by a servant and a carriage. We had a hurried dinner so as to accompany the Dowager Empress and her children to the Champ de Mars, which we drove round several times. The crowd of carriages and pedestrians was even bigger than the day before. It is the only time the Russian people seem a little festive. About a score of court carriages drove the girls of Smol'nyi and the Empress's Institutes round the ice mountains. They were piled up eight to ten in every carriage. The next day all these pleasures had disappeared.

The following two days, already Russian Lent, still afforded some amusements for foreigners. They are called the foreign carnival. There was a masked ball for them in the Grand Theatre, where only men went. On the morning of Tuesday 22nd we got the first news of the terrible floods of the 3rd and 4th in the Netherlands. We spent the rest of the week quietly at home. All the Russians were at their devotions and receiving no one.

March

Tuesday, March 1st. We received confirmation of the bad news of the floods in Holland. The Princess gave us the Prince's letter to read and assured us that his first action would be to return home at once to help the sufferers. The Grand Duke Michael came in at that moment and asked her if she wanted to give the sea a kick, since she could do nothing by her presence.

Tuesday, March 8th. I had a sleigh drive with Mama in the delightful weather which had already lasted several days, which was five degrees of frost and a beautiful warm sun. We crossed the river on the ice, something I had long wanted to do, first to Vassil'evskii ostrov and then to the Fortress. The driving was detestable, with bumpy ice furrowed in many places by the constant passage of sleighs even in the periods of thaw. We drove into the Fortress and after going round inside the walls, recrossed the river and took another drive through the streets.

Wednesday, March 9th. The Minister of Foreign Affairs, Count Nesselrode, informed the Emperor and the Princess of the news that the Prince of Orange was to leave Brussels that very day. The Princess absolutely refused to believe it and kept on repeating that the Prince would probably not come back at all if he could be of any help to the victims of the floods.

Mama and I had been invited a week before to dine that day with Countess Stroganov, the daughter of Princess Vladimir Golitsyn. We arrived about four o'clock. Like most of the ancient Russian families, this lady keeps open house when she dines at home, which is only twice a week since she dines with her mother every other day. A certain number of places are set and anyone who wishes may come. Countess Stroganov's house is a real palace on the corner of the Nevskii Prospect and the Moika canal.[1] While waiting for dinner the Countess showed us round the house. She began with her father-in-law's collections, including a fine collection of pictures which is open to the public in the mornings. Then we saw her private rooms

[1] The baroque Stroganov Palace was built in 1752-4 by Rastrelli, with many rooms decorated by Voronikhin. The palace, with one of the best art collections in Russia, was kept by the family until the Revolution. The collection was largely transferred to the Hermitage.

with every possible luxury, including a delicious bathroom. We were oddly seated at dinner. The table was very long and narrow with Princess Vladimir at the head, Mama on her left and next to her the mistress of the house. Then came Count de Maistre and a series of young people, mostly officers, sons-in-law, nephews and cousins of the Countess. I was placed between a great-grandmother and a grandmother, Princess Vladimir and another of her daughters, Countess Apraksin, who had come from Moscow to pay her mother a visit. Next came Countess Stroganov's daughters and nieces, followed by a string of young female companions with a couple of old duennas. The dinner was much the same as we got at court. There was much talk of Moscow, and Mme Apraksin invited us to come and see her there. She is one of Moscow's leading hostesses. We stayed till after seven, and on our return learned of the arrival of Grand Duke Nicholas and his wife from Berlin. At half past eleven the cannon from the Fortress announced the birth of the Grand Duchess Maria Mikhailovna or 'Michael's daughter'.

Thursday, March 10th. A Te Deum was sung for this happy birth. We went in Russian dresses and the singing was glorious. Afterwards the Princess received the gentlemen who had come to congratulate her. They included General Chernyshev, who could think of nothing better than to talk to the Princess of the Prince's imminent arrival. He had chosen an unfortunate subject. We were doing crewel work at the end of the room and were very much amused to hear this famous talker put down by the answer he got. 'Perhaps the Prince is coming back but I personally know nothing about it, and I know him well enough to know that he will always prefer duty to pleasure.' The great Chernyshev did not know what to reply. He took refuge in retreat, and we teased him a lot about it at dinner when he came to eat with us.

Friday, March 11th. Mama was busy and asked the Princess to take me with her on her round of visits. This gave me the honour of encountering the Emperor, who found us all chatting in the Diamond Salon with his brother Nicholas. The Princess and the Grand Duchess Maria, who turned up afterwards, embraced the Emperor with a tenderness which was really suffocating, but he managed to say a few words to me with his usual amiability. The Grand Duchess Maria went back to her apartment after the Princess had left to go to her mother. No sooner had she reached the door when she asked me to request her brother Nicholas, with whom she was to dine, for leave to dress in his palace after her afternoon drive. I do not know why she could not ask this question in her sister's presence, but retraced my steps and found the brothers in the reigning Empress's bedroom. The Emperor asked if I was going back to my apartment, and I answered that I had a message for the Grand Duke and passed it on at once. The Emperor talked a little and then they left me.

When I had finished my duty with the Princess I got into a sleigh with Pauline, and we were joined by M. van Heeckeren and M. de Lagrené, an attaché at the French Embassy. They were to take us to a garden outside the city where there was an ice mountain for the upper classes, but when we reached the city gate our coachman refused to drive us through. Our servant explained that the Prince Dolgorukii, the Master of the Horse, had expressly ordered that no court carriage was to drive beyond the city gates.[2] We had no notion that we were prisoners in the city, all the more since I had been to 'Krasnyi kabak' with Mlle Kochetov a few days previously. Pauline however managed to persuade the servants that Dolgorukii knew of our excursion (which was quite untrue) and we succeeded in reaching our destination.

We got out at a little pavilion where there were refreshments for anyone who wanted them, and then went straight on to the ice mountains which were facing one another close by. They are watered every evening so that the ice stays perfectly smooth.

[2] The Grand Duke Constantine arrived this day from Warsaw for a short stay, during which he met as few people as possible. There was no celebration and Dolgorukii's unexpected order may have proceeded from the wish to keep the visit quiet.

M. de Lagrené was very clever at going down himself and sending other people down as well. You put on a huge pair of red leather gloves because you have to steer your sledge by hand. Pauline soon decided to have a try, and then repeated it several times. As for myself I did not venture, especially once I had seen the thing close to and heard the ladies scream when the descent was at its fastest. Even the ones who love this exercise will tell you they have the feeling of being thrown out of the window, and this is not an idea that appealed to me. So I continued walking up and down in the snow, along with several mothers, who had brought their daughters. If you do not insist on being sent flying by a gentleman, there are peasants standing by to do the job professionally, who are clever experts, but most of the young ladies let themselves be frozen and bored rather than use a 'muzhik'. They wait there patiently for a partner to invite them, as at dances. We stayed there a full hour in fine cold weather, and it was a new experience to walk up and down a frozen snow-covered canal. We dined with Mme Hogguer with some gentlemen and spent the evening at Princess Vladimir Golitsyn's. Prince Dolgorukii was there and knew about our morning escapade already, but Pauline spoke to him and all passed off smoothly.

Monday, March 14th. There was a far bigger crowd than usual to watch the Emperor leave the morning parade, perhaps because the Imperial family was there in force. All three Grand Dukes, including Constantine, were present. Later the three of us were free so we went out walking on the English Quay and met the Emperor and the Princess. This was a great condescension on His Majesty's part as he likes to walk about incognito, yet out of consideration for his lady sister was being followed by a carriage. I did not see the Princess again until March 30th.

That evening the wooden theatre caught fire. It had only lately been transported from Oranienbaum by order of General Miloradovich. Fortunately because of Lent there was no performance there. The theatre was completely burnt down in a matter of hours, and from our windows we could see the flames over the rooftops. They say the spectacle was magnificent, if melancholy, and many people drove along the other side of the Fontanka canal to watch it. In spite of the excessive heat they managed to save the neighbouring buildings and the stores of wood and merchandise near by. In St Petersburg no one works to put out fires except trained firefighters. They are a large corps drilled like a special army. Among other things they are taught to throw themselves from third or fourth floor windows into blankets which their comrades hold to catch them. Some of them usually die in every fire, for they are disciplined to take all risks. In this fire three of them disappeared without a trace, but no one mentioned them and when I spoke of it to someone he replied, 'That is their battle. They go into it like other soldiers into action. We do not talk of it.'

Tuesday, March 15th. We took a walk along the Fontanka so as took look on the remnants of the theatre. We met M. Kavelin who helped us to get through the crowd of curious onlookers. As we walked along he told us that the fire was a real blessing, because sooner or later there would have been a frightful accident. There was only one exit and it was impossible to open the boxes from inside. We could not avoid dining with Countess Protassov, the senior maid of honour, who combines the misfortune of blindness with that of being extremely discontented with her fate, though everyone tries to make things as easy as possible for her. She is revolting in her habits and has earned the nickname 'Lady of the Lake', because, as Pauline says, she cannot contain her sluices and sometimes floods the floor. At eight we went to a charming party at Princess Meshcherskii's, where a Lancer officer, an exquisite composer, let us hear his talented compositions. The dry heat is so great in our rooms that the furniture cracks, my hair stays curled all day and Pauline maintains that we are getting smaller. I am small enough already.

Wednesday, March 16th. Pauline and I wanted to visit Mlle Nelidov who lives with her niece in an apartment in the Smol'nyi convent, where the community of noble ladies is established. Our visit was fruitless, as they were not at home, except in that we were able to see into the convent courtyard with its unfinished church, which looks as if it is falling into ruins. They say it would cost as much to demolish it as to complete it. The cupolas are gilded. The Empress Elizabeth had it built along with the convent where she hoped to end her days.[3]

Saturday, March 19th. General Chernyshev came to fetch us, Pauline, Mlle Kochetov and me, for a visit to the Academy of Sciences.[4] The Academy is near the Bourse in the Vassil'evskii ostrov quarter. Fortunately we had our fur cloaks because it was very cold. We began with fossils, then meteorites which had fallen all over Russia, and a collection of Russian minerals, then a planetary system and much natural history preserved in spirit. Among the vessels were two skeletons wearing little green taffeta skirts for reasons of decency. One belonged to a stoker or *istopnik* with only two fingers, the other to one of Peter the Great's Heiduks, a real colossus. Then there is a large room full of stuffed quadrupeds, among them a bear killed in the neighbourhood of St Petersburg, and, most remarkable of all, the skeleton of a mammoth, the most complete ever discovered, sent there by Mlle Glasenapp's father. The animal is so huge that an elephant seems small beside it. It has two horns or quasi-tusks on each side of its mouth. There were a number of curiosities connected with Peter the Great: first of all some objects he had turned on a lathe, the lathe itself, then some copper plates he had engraved, his geometrical instruments and carpenter's tools, plans, little models of ships, even a pair of spectacles. Also there was his desk at which he used to write standing up, so high that General Chernyshev could hardly reach it, the horse he rode

[3] The Smol'nyi convent was founded in 1748 and designed by Rastrelli. However work on the buildings was slow owing to lack of funds. The convent itself closed in 1797 and the buildings were turned into a home for noble widows. The Institute was founded in 1764 by Catherine the Great for daughters of the gentry, but was moved from the convent into a building designed by Quarenghi, which was supported by the Empress Maria Fedorovna.

[4] Founded in 1724 by Peter the Great, the present building was built by Quarenghi in 1783-9.

at the Battle of Poltava, stuffed, two of his dogs and a little greyhound which once brought him a petition. Finally there was a plaster death-mask taken a few instants after his death, which was used to help in modelling a large wax figure dressed in the Tsar's garments in a neighbouring closet. A nail fixed in the door gives the Tsar's height; he was enormously tall. The walls are covered with portraits of the whole Romanov family, including Catherine I. Her physiognomy shows clearly what she was before she married the great ruler. Last of all they showed us a book kept in a well-guarded sanctuary. It contained some of Catherine II's ideas, including a project for a law on capital punishment. Her supreme court abolished the death penalty but allowed a man to be beaten with the knout until he expired under its lashes.[5]

That evening we visited the Grand Duchess Alexandrine.[6] She was a new acquaintance for me and her state of health – she was pregnant – did not allow me to admire her figure, which they say, is like our Queen's.[7] She received us in a charming little salon furnished in the Russian style. She was smartly dressed in a white satin frock cut high, a pretty hat and a red cashmere shawl. Her husband is very anxious for her to be always well turned out. She seemed a little tongue-tied because she lacks the flow of honeyed chatter of the Russian Grand Duchesses, but what she says seems more natural. When we had left her we called on Mme Stroganov, and on returning heard from Pauline that the Prince of Orange had arrived.[8]

Sunday, March 20th. Neither that day nor Monday did we see the Prince. We saw the Emperor's doctor, Dr Wylie, at dinner. He is an outspoken Englishman who talks frankly and

[5] In fact the death penalty had been abolished by Elizabeth in 1753.

[6] Alexandra Fedorovna, the wife of Grand Duke Nicholas.

[7] They were both Prussian princesses.

[8] After a record journey of ten days and eighteen hours from Brussels the Prince had returned against his wife's wishes. This perhaps explains hints of awkwardness and coldness in their court recorded in the journal. It was four days before Cornélie saw the Prince, while the Princess did not see her for eighteen days, perhaps because she did not think it funny to be laughed at.

is very knowledgeable in his profession. He has taken a great fancy to us, especially to Mama, whom he never calls anything but Countess Wismar.

Tuesday, March 22nd. At last we encountered the Prince on the Quay where he was taking a walk like us, and on the next day he paid us a visit in our apartment, to break the ice as he expressed himself. I was by myself and he stayed to talk for a moment, then came back next day to see the ladies.

Wednesday, March 23. The anniversary of the death of Emperor Paul. All the court was in mourning and the Dowager Empress took all her children to visit her husband's tomb.

Thursday, March 24th. The day of Emperor Alexander's accession. All the courtiers who approached Their Highnesses were in gala dress, but the Imperial family themselves were dressed as simply as possible, and there was no celebration. The city was illuminated in an odd manner, with all the edges of the sidewalks lit up with street lamps but none of the houses. That evening we paid calls, something that was becoming almost impossible and extremely tiring because of the bad state of the streets. The thaw had started several days before but had not yet completely melted the heavy crust of snow and ice covering the roadway. Also the paving had been damaged in the flood and was coming to pieces here and there, which made the streets, especially the Nevskii Prospect, a real death trap for carriages. Colonels Buturlin and Glasenapp called on us that evening. Buturlin's conversation is very agreable. He is almost the only Russian of my acquaintance who knows how to talk.

Sunday, March 27th. I went to church alone and when I came back found the Prince with all his suite in the corridor, watching for the moment when the Emperor starts for the daily morning parade, so as to be able to accompany him.

Tuesday, March 29th. There was a wretched incident, almost without precedent in the Russian army – an NCO stabbed his captain to death. They say the captain had driven him to despair. For fear that such conduct prove contagious the punishment was exemplary. As the death penalty does not exist, the miserable fellow was condemned to 4,000 lashes, to be followed by transportation to Siberia, a meaningless addition to his sentence. The sentence was carried out a few days later by the Guards regiment and, once the 4,000 lashes were inflicted, there was nothing left of him but a mass of lifeless flesh.

Thursday, March 31st. Nothing of interest to relate; our quiet life goes on as usual and I have not seen the Princess for eighteen days. The weather has been splendid but everything is covered with snow. Our coachman, who had been to Kronstadt yesterday, about twenty miles from St Petersburg, told us the ice was three to four feet thick on the river and the gulf was frozen several miles beyond the port.

April

Sunday, April 3rd. Our Easter Sunday, the Grand Duchess Maria Mikhailovna was baptised. At half past ten we presented ourselves to the Princess in full Russian dress with all accessories. Thence we proceeded to the Service Hall where soon the whole Imperial family filed past with the exception of the reigning Empress and the Grand Duchesses Alexandrine and Elena. The Emperor conducted his mother, the Prince of Orange the Grand Duchess Maria, and the Prince of Saxe-Weimar the Princess of Orange. Then came the Grand Duke Nicholas, the two young Princes of Saxe-Weimar and the infant, carried by the Grand Duchess Elena's Mistress of the Robes, Countess El'mpt, supported on each side by Prince Kurakin and Admiral Mordvinov, and finally the whole court as usual.

The Imperial family this time stood inside the grille dividing the chapel so that we could get nearer and see better. The font and a small altar had been placed in front of the sanctuary, the Emperor stood on the left of the entrance to the grille, the Empress on the right, each with a taper in their hands, and with the child between them. They began by turning her back on the altar so that she could spit, then they rubbed her with oil presented by the Emperor. The Emperor's confessor, an impressive old man, then baptised her. They cut a little of the infant's hair, and the priest, stopping her ears, mouth and nose with his fingers, plunged her three times in the font. The Empress received her in a heavy towel and handed her to Countess El'mpt, who, aided by a servant, dried her, wrapped her up again and gave her back to the Empress. She then took her in her arms and walked three times round the altar, followed by the Emperor who had some trouble in avoiding walking on her train. When that was over, the infant was carried behind a screen in the corner of the chapel, where the wet nurse, the nurserymaids and midwife were waiting to dress her. Once she was clothed the Grand Duke Michael, who according to Greek ritual could not be present at the christening and had had to stay outside the church all this time, reappeared to thank the Emperor and Empress, who embraced him. After this the Mass began with the Metropolitan of Novgorod officiating. When the moment of Communion approached the Empress went back behind the screen to fetch the little girl. She was by this time dressed in silver brocade and lying on a gold brocade cushion. The Empress had the infant given Communion and, after returning her to Countess El'mpt, decorated her with the Order of St Catherine. The Mass finished soon afterwards – about half past one. The chants had been superb.

The Imperial family retired to their apartments, which gave us a short rest before the dinner given by the Emperor, announced for two o'clock. We therefore went to one of the salons overlooking the river where everyone met. The clergy were there too, including the Catholic bishop, an old man of ninety, the Uniat Bishop, the Metropolitans of Kiev and Novgorod, and the Empress's confessor. Everyone kissed their hands, an honour they value, and they in turn gave blessings, making the Sign of the Cross over each person who kissed their hands. After rather a long wait the Marshal of the

Court placed everyone according to their rank at the table in the Great Hall, where we had supped after the White Hall ball. A horseshoe table occupied its length, but was not quite filled up. We sat down when the Imperial family had entered. Throughout dinner there was excellent music from the gallery round the room, which was only interrupted by the fanfares when a health was drunk to the accompaniment of the cannon firing from the Fortress. The dinner was as bad as possible for our heretic stomachs. It was entirely Lenten fare because of the attendant clergy. The only good dish I tasted was sterlet, a very expensive fish of exquisite flavour.[1] After dinner everyone went home to rest from the day's fatigues. The diplomatic corps were present at the baptism but not the dinner, except for the Prince of Hohenlohe as minister for Württemberg. He walked about among the courtiers like a scabby sheep, but they were too prudent to converse with him.

Friday, April 8th. Good Friday. Countess Fritsch invited us to visit several other churches with her. We began with the Armenians, where we heard a long and very pathetic-sounding sermon of which we did not understand a word. Thence to the church of Malta which is Catholic, where we found the candles all extinguished, a black catafalque and some people praying. Finally we went to the Kazan' Cathedral where a coffin was exposed to be kissed, while the faithful lit small tapers before it. Not much impressed with these excursions, we went home.

Saturday, April 9th. Mama and I went to bed at six in the evening so as to get ready for the famous Easter night. I did not sleep at all but felt fresh and ready to put on my best and grandest dress. They fired cannon shots at half past nine, eleven and half past eleven. We then went to the Service Hall where soon another cannon shot announced midnight. The Imperial family appeared, went to the chapel and soon reappeared in a procession with the priests. The court stayed in the church and everyone was given a lighted candle. There were

[1] A species of small sturgeon.

[100]

very few ladies present. After some minutes the procession returned with very beautiful chants. Colonel Apraksin and M. Kavelin were behind us and sang in unison with the choir, when they were not chattering to one another. After a good hour the candles were put out to my great joy, because mine was bothering me very much. The service as a whole lasted till half past two, counting the greetings the Emperor received from the Council only. Formerly he used to receive them from all the men present, who came to embrace him and to kiss the Empress's hand. This meant the service was considerably shortened. As soon as all Their Highnesses had departed everyone embraced everyone else, saying 'Christ is risen', for the Russians congratulate one another on every occasion. When they have taken Communion they embrace again, and a high-born lady cannot refuse to embrace her coachman, bearded though he may be. I had nothing more interesting to embrace than my pillow.

Sunday, April 10th. We put on Russian dresses before dinner so as to be in the Service Hall at half past four to kiss the Empress's hand. This used to take place in the chapel after Vespers, but the Emperor's leg prevents him standing for so long, so it was done this time before his arrival. This made the ceremony much less imposing then we had expected. The ladies advanced in some confusion and turned their backs upon the Empress after kissing her hand, instead of retiring backwards for some paces. The Emperor appeared when this was over.

Monday, April 11th. I stayed at home to let Mama and our companions go to church while I went with the Princess to see the Empress. On the way back she asked me to go to Mass, adding that she would let me know when it was time to go — without telling me I should have to dress for it. So when they came to call me I appeared in hat and morning frock and found the Princess all dressed up. She looked quite frightened when she saw me but remembered she had not warned me, saying I had plenty of time to get into a suitable dress. I ran off remembering that our maids would not have returned from church. I considered taking a dress with me and begging one of the Princess's women to help me, when I found Pauline was back and she came to my aid. I wore a toque with diamonds I had worn the day before and got into some shoes. The whole proceeding took less than ten minutes, and I was back with the Princess in good time for Mass. When it was over I accompanied her to the reigning Empress's. After bringing her back I fetched Mama and Pauline who were to join us for the farewell audience of the English minister, Mr Canning. The reigning Empress dined that day with the Imperial family for the first time since her illness.

Among the Easter traditions I had almost forgotten to mention the custom of giving porcelain eggs as presents. The Emperor sent a very beautiful one to each of us in a little basket with a cup. The Dowager Empress gave us each a smaller one, and the Princess gave a pretty malachite clock to Mama, a malachite inkstand to me, and a fine present to Pauline.

Wednesday, April 13th. As no one could come with me I went alone to call on the Nelidov ladies in the Smol'nyi convent. I was received this time and found them in very pretty rooms, especially the niece's. Out of her window I could see a fir tree in the convent garden and this gave me great pleasure. I was aching to see green trees. There was a lot of wind on my drive back, the water was rising and carriages were forbidden to cross the river, although pedestrians were still doing so. We paid some more calls in the evening and then went to Mme Naryshkin's, whose nameday it was. She had a little party, where, among others, was a Spaniard of the name of Saur [*sic*], who is a celebrated performer on the guitar.[2] He played a delightful fantasy of a hunt, in which you could clearly hear the gallop of horses and the sound of horns as if an orchestra were playing. His vocal accompaniment was not so good, his voice almost nothing and his French pronunciation disagreeable. I regret the end of Lent because parties and balls are

[2] Fernando Sor, the Catalan guitarist (1778-1839).

starting again everywhere, and I fear the court will soon be setting us going as well.

Thursday, April 14th. It has been thawing for eight days but the Neva is still frozen and there is not a sign of spring. I would give two ducats to see a single tree in leaf. Of course the hothouses give us a great deal. We have been eating asparagus, spinach and lettuces for a long time, and there was a small plate of fresh cherries at the christening dinner, but nothing to replace our lovely nature as we have it in April and May. On Easter Day I saw a basket of strawberries at the Princess's which scented the whole room. We had dinner with the Dowager Empress. At Mama's request, made through the Princess, she was good enough to give us gracious leave to visit her Institutes, and told us she had ordered her secretary, M. Novosil'tsev, to accompany us. Some time ago it had been hinted we should ask for this permission, as the Empress likes people to look at her establishments. We were not spared the inspection of a single one, except the Institute of St Catherine where there was measles.

Friday, April 15th. M. Novosil'tsev came to pick us up at ten and took us to a school for guardsmen's daughters. The headmistress, a German speaker, has sixty-six pupils who spend the day at school and lodge at home. They are taught religion, Russian, reading and writing. Their handiwork — woven embroideries, gloves and shoes — is sold on their behalf. Their food is very good and very neatly served. Next we visited a school for the daughters of officers below the rank of major-general in the Guards. The headmistress speaks French as well as German. She has one hundred noble and fifty middle-class pupils. They all learn writing, reading and religion, but the former learn French as well as German, the latter only German. They took us to the dining room where they all sit down together since the flood, because the middle-class girls had had to move. They were all drawn up with their hair plaited almost too elegantly for everyday. I think they must have taken special trouble for us. They sang grace before sitting down to table, which is the rule in all the Empress's Institutes, but there is nothing very edifying about it.

We then went on to the Incurables where I dreaded seeing some appalling diseases, but most of the patients were blind. There are about forty men engaged in making mats and corks, and twenty women knitting and sewing. Their work is sold on their behalf. When we had seen their dormitories, which were very clean, their pretty chapel and their garden, we found them all together in their dining room. The men sang grace rather discordantly, then they made us taste their soup and beef and gruel, all well cooked. The head of this establishment talks very good German and French and has a pleasant face. From there we went to another school for soldiers' daughters, founded two years ago, and managed for the Empress by a number of ladies who take turns to supervise the daily work there. Mme Zakrevskii, the wife of the governor of Finland, was on duty that day. That was the end of our first day's excursions.

Saturday, April 16th. M. Novosil'tsev took us to the Foundling Hospital, an enormous building where 1,100 people are fed daily. We found the same director who was at the Incurables. Infants are received by the head porter who simply asks if they have been baptised. He gives a numbered card to the person who brought the child, and the number is recorded so that those who wish can get their children back after a certain time. The child is bathed, put into swaddling clothes and given to one of the wet nurses, who are always standing by in readiness. The nurse is fed and lodged, and paid 250 roubles for her trouble. There were 470 infants in the place the day we went, put in different rooms with their wet nurses, all of whom are hideous though very clean. There is the greatest cleanliness everywhere and they assured us this is always so. The Empress frequently makes unexpected visits of inspection. When the children have spent several months here they are boarded out with peasants all round St Petersburg and stay there until the age of ten. They are then placed in the foundling hospital at Gatchina, another of the Empress's foundations. After several years there they return to this one, where, according to their abilities, they are taught a trade or prepared for the Academy. As for the girls they either become servants in an Institute, dressmakers, governesses or midwives. After seeing all the tiny children we inspected all the classrooms for the various crafts – printers, cobblers, tailors, joiners, toolmakers etc.

We then went to the classrooms which prepare the children for the Academy. Two boards are hung there, one with black edges, the other red. The first contains the names of those who have been lazy in their studies, the second those of diligent pupils. I was assured the first was almost always empty. After the pharmacy, the chapel and the library we visited the dormitory for midwives, all girls of fifteen to seventeen. The famous gynaecologist, M. Dutov, selects them from young pupils of the house and prepares them very early for instruction in a sort of college. They start by bleeding women who are secretly confined here. The Empress has set rooms aside for women of all classes who desire to keep a strict incognito. She visits them herself but does not let any of her ladies go with her. This establishment is as much a good work as the system by which any child can be deposited in the Institute, but both of them give rise to serious abuses. Many low-class women leave their infants with the porter and then offer themselves as wet nurses. Thus they are paid for feeding their own child, and then show their number and remove the child. But to return to the student midwives, they are given places in the provinces when they have delivered eighty women in the Institute. The Empress wants the provinces to be well provided for. The pupil governesses are also placed outside the capital. The Russian nobles in the capital do not think these girls are good enough and prefer foreign women to bring up their children, although the Institute teaches all subjects required for a good governess, as well as dressmaking, embroidery and dancing.

Having admired all we had seen, we thanked the director

and drove off to visit the Institute for the deaf and dumb. This establishment is still in its infancy. The head, a gentle, pleasant-looking woman, sent for the inmates, not more than twenty cheerful, contented-looking girls, talking to one another in sign language, something that spreads an atmosphere of frightened silence round them for people who are not accustomed to it. They had a fairly animated conversation among themselves. I think we were the subject of it, for I saw them laugh and look at us while they were talking with their fingers with surprising speed. The head is very anxious to have a teacher from our Institute at Groningen to teach these children.[3]

Monday, April 18th. We started with a new establishment for victims of the flood, 160 of them, mothers and children. We were present at their four-course dinner, a menu they think proper for the officers' widows in the house. We tasted it and I thought it was better than the food they gave us in the palace. From there we visited the Pauper Hospital, a magnificent building in the Liteinyi Prospect.[4] It can hold 300 patients, and when we visited there were 260. On the ground floor you find two pharmacies, one for women and one for men, where free medication is handed to all paupers with certificates to show they cannot pay. We were exempted from visiting some twenty wards for putrid fevers and nerve cases, but could not escape the doctors' consultation room with its wax models of every sort of affliction, which had been cured or at least treated in this place. We passed these hideous things as fast as possible, as well as the operating theatre equipped with all its instruments. They say that in important cases the Empress watches the operation and encourages the patient by her presence and words.

Tuesday, April 19th. To finish all our visits we went to the the House for Noble Ladies, the twin Institute of St Catherine's

[3] The Institute for the Deaf and Dumb at Groningen was founded in 1785 by Pastor H.D. Guyot and was internationally famous.

[4] The Maria Hospital, built by Quarenghi in 1803–5 in classical style.

on the Fontanka, which we could not visit because of measles in the house. This community inhabits the old Smol'nyi convent, founded by the Empress Elizabeth, who had intended to end her days here but could not carry out her wish. She had not even finished the church in the centre of the buildings, which form a great rectangle with several inner courts. This church would have been magnificent. It is several stories high and has five gilded cupolas, but there are only four outer walls without doors or windows. They say it would cost as much to demolish as to complete, with the result that it is left unfinished. It is a long time since this convent has been inhabited by nuns, but the directress of the Institute still bears the title of Mother Superior. Mme Adlerberg, lady of honour to the Empresses, holds this position, and her court rank is purely honorary, for she hardly ever appears there. She has the most winning amiable manners and a fine apartment in the newest part of the building, added to the original convent by the Dowager Empress. Twelve young female pupils dine with her every day.

The community is divided into two, noble and middle class. Each of them has its own refectory and dormitories. We were received in the middle-class refectory by a lady who looks after it under Mme Adlerberg. In the first form we met M. Herman, the principal teacher of the Institute, who gives lessons to the girls in a most paternal manner. He examined them in our presence in the first elements of geography and history. The best pupils form the so-called 'nursery seed-bed [*pépinière*]'. They wear grey dresses and give elementary lessons to the little ones, thus preparing themselves to become assistant teachers or governesses. One of them is always attached to the Mother Superior to carry her orders to the various classes and to accompany her on inspections. The girl attached to her today looked very pleasant but was so extremely timid that she was hardly able to answer our questions.

To reach the noble quarters we had to go to the opposite end of the building and on the way saw two more establishments. First was St Mary's Institute which had been given refuge in the Smol'nyi since the flood. Young people are brought up there to become maidservants or dressmakers. Next was the Widows' Institute, some of whose members we had already seen nursing patients. These women are only admitted after proving that they have no other means of subsistence, and that their husbands have had ten years' blameless service to their credit as officers. It follows that they are not very numerous. At last we reached the quarters of girls of noble birth. There is a small room at each end of every dormitory, one occupied by the class mistress, the other by two young servant girls, recruited from the Foundling Hospital. In the corridors we met Mlle Nelidov (the niece) with Mlle Baranov, Mme Adlerberg's granddaughter. They accompanied us through the various noble classes, distinguished by the colour of their dresses, brown, blue, green according to age. The two senior classes had been amalgamated so as to shorten our tour a little. Mme Adlerberg served us chocolate, after which there was a long examination in Russian and general history. M. Herman asked all the questions, giving a lot of attention to the influence of geography and climate on the civilisation of nations. An assumption that was rather strange to us was that the barbarism of the Middle Ages was due to lack of paper. A girl then played the piano and others sang in chorus but, their master being absent, they lost their way a little. Mme Adlerberg was the first to notice this.

While this was going on, Mme Adlerberg had had all the pupils of the Institute, noble as well as middle class, assembled in a pillared hall where they have their final examination. As we approached, the double doors flew open and the young girls, all drawn up by classes with the little ones in front, curtsied to us in unison like a field of barley bowing in the wind. I must admit I was a little embarrassed as I returned their greeting, feeling that all eyes were fixed on us. We toured the hall and were shown some handiwork, probably so as to give the girls the time to take their seats in the refectory, where we were taken later. The girls stood and sang their grace harmoniously. Their dinner was fairly large and probably a bit more sumptuous than usual to do us honour. The potatoes in particular were better than any I had previously seen in Russia. I in fact ate a good big portion as I was dying of hunger. Remember it was three o'clock and we had been walking round this Institute since ten. We then said goodbye to Mme Adlerberg and thanked her for her kindness.

We did not get back to the palace until half past three, too late to go to dinner with the Empress to which all of us had been invited. The day before Mama should have dined there and had returned in time, but the Princess was afraid she might have brought back some infection from the Pauper Hospital and told her she need not come. To hide this piece of childishness from the Empress, who had seen M. Novosil'tsev and knew that we were back, the Princess told her that Mama preferred to stay at home so as to see the Neva ice break. The ice did break that day but we saw nothing of it. Mama took care the Empress should know what really happened by relating the whole thing to Countess Lieven.

Wednesday, April 20th. We continued our instructive sightseeing in St Petersburg by visiting the Convent of St Alexander Nevskii.[5] Our servant Ivan showed us round, explaining to the best of his ability the information given by a sort of sacristan. One enters the convent by a gate preceded by a bridge, as in a fortress, and inside there is a courtyard planted with trees. The Metropolitan's palace is on one side opposite the church, which has a pillared portico. The monks are lodged in the side buildings. First we saw a separate chapel used for burying uncrowned members of the Romanov dynasty. Two of the Emperor Alexander's daughters are buried here. The chief St Petersburg families have their vaults alongside, with monuments or inscribed flat stones. The Emperor's place within the church is on a sort of crimson velvet dais, standing against a column with a portrait of Empress Catherine above it and one

[5] Founded in 1718. The domed archway was built by Starov in 1783-85 but most of the original buildings were by Trezzini. The Metropolitan's house was by Rastorguev (1756-9).

Emperor Peter III below. Another picture represents the conversion of the reigning Empress, surrounded by the whole Imperial family; it is an absolute daub. The finest treasure is the reliquary of St Alexander Nevskii, the Grand Prince of Russia [Novgorod] surnamed Nevskii for his victory over the Swedes on the Neva. It is made of solid silver and weighs a total of 10,000 pounds.[6] The Imperial family only comes to services here on very great occasions.

Thursday, April 21st. We took a liberty we had never previously taken while in St Petersburg. We went for a walk without a servant or carriage in attendance, the sort of suite which always bored us very much. We were not quite certain if we would be allowed to do this but did it often afterwards without the slightest bother.

Friday, April 22nd. Mlle Kochetov accompanied us to the Tauride Palace at the east end of the city.[7] The Empress Catherine built it for her favourite Prince Potemkin. The Emperor Paul turned it into a riding school and the Emperor Alexander has had it restored. We saw the preparations, still in progress, for a splendid celebration, first intended for the marriage of Grand Duke Michael, and then for our arrival in the city, which had been cancelled by the sad events of the winter. Enormous scaffolding had been built outside to let off fireworks and to seat spectators. Inside, a grandiose hall, its roof supported by two double rows of eighteen columns each, had its whole ceiling hung with gold and silver garlands made of shining silver foil. Lustres hung from it formed of crowns of leaves supporting silvered candlesticks. The columns were hung in the same way and ornaments representing Hymen's torches lined the walls, and led up to a red glass urn lit from within. There was a covered garden, separated from the open garden by a double screen of glass, and from the Great Hall by a row of

[6] Now in the Hermitage.

[7] The Tauride Palace, in what was then a sparsely populated area of the city, was built by Starov in 1783-9 and so named for Potemkin's conquest and annexation of the Crimea.

columns. You walk on sanded paths past verdant lanes not broken up by flower beds but edged with orange trees, box hedges, little fir trees and small shrubs, which form attractive groves where you can rest on benches. Coloured glass houses, cleverly placed in these plantations, would have been lit up from inside, and everything would have combined to make this festival into fairyland. We very much regretted we never saw it. We also visited the huge hothouses which are well worth seeing. We went through several, full of peach trees, pear and plum trees all in blossom, apricot trees with fruit already formed, vines with ripe grapes, and fig trees. I could not breathe in the pineapple house, as the temperature stood at twenty-two degrees Réaumur [81.50 Fahrenheit]. All the trees in these hothouses looked well-grown and strong but their fruits are generally rather insipid.

Tuesday, April 26th. The temperature stood at fourteen degrees above zero [63.5 Fahrenheit]. Mama went for a drive with the Princess, and Pauline and I went for a walk.

Wednesday, April 27th. I went to the play in the Nevskii Prospect theatre with Countess Eglofstein. We thought we were going to break our ribs before we got there, the thaw had damaged the pavement so badly.

Thursday, April 28th. A nightingale was singing at the top of its voice in the Dowager Empress's rooms. I found this lovely singing indoors saddening, all the more so because there was not a single sign of spring, although the season was so forward.[8]

May

Tuesday, May 3rd. The Prince left for Moscow in the evening. He came to take leave of us but found only me at home.

[8] In a letter to Agatha Cornélie wrote nostalgically: 'If only you knew how often I am hovering round you, walking through the rooms at Ruurlo, going so far as to climb into your bed, walking by moonlight in the garden, listening to the nightingales. Sometimes I am wandering in the park at Twickel, in my boudoir or among my pictures.'

Wednesday, May 4th. The weather got a little milder. We took tea with the Princess in the evening and I walked with her next day (5th). We went to the Summer Garden where they were working to repair the damage done by the flood and put the paths in order. Here and there the grass was beginning to grow but there was hardly enough for a goat's breakfast. The river was full of blocks of ice, and a shower of rain ended the Princess's walk. All three of us dined that evening with Countess Orlov-Chesmenskii. The company was very agreeable including General Benckendorff and his wife, Countesses El'mpt and Fritsch etc. There were a great many courses. They began with oysters, then two kinds of hot soup, followed by a cold soup which was green like vegetable soup but made of *kvass* [a Russian beverage] with pieces of fish floating in it. This was followed by a fish pie, a very heavy kind of pastry which may be eaten in Lent. Countess Orlov eats Lenten food all the year round. Next came the beef, well cooked like all the rest of the dinner. M. Orlov, the Countess's cousin, helped her to do the honours. She has been very kind to this man and has often paid his debts. People would like her to marry him, but she has constantly refused all thought of marriage.

Sunday, May 8th. In the morning the reigning Empress sent us three little baskets of strawberries and raspberries.

Monday, May 9th. There was a dinner for 150 at the Dowager Empress's in honour of Grand Duke Constantine's birthday. The Emperor was not there, having left a few days earlier for Warsaw. We met in the Service Hall, where the Empress held a circle both before and after dinner. Dinner was in the large square salon between the Grand Duchess Maria's apartment and the Dowager Empress's. Present were the higher clergy, and there was charming music.

Tuesday, May 10th. We went shopping in the morning with one of the Hogguers and there was a very cold wind. We wanted a few pretty things to take home, not at all easy to do since there is very little in the St Petersburg shops and anything passable costs a king's ransom.

Wednesday, May 11th. All three of us accompanied the Princess to the Academies of Sciences and Arts, with Prince Cherbatov also in the party. We had already been there in March with General Chernyshev, but they showed us several things we had not seen before. A M. Uvarov received the Princess and conducted her round, even to the observatory at the top of the building, where a violent wind prevented us from spending much time in enjoying the lovely view of the whole city at our feet, and the full breadth of the Neva. They showed us various objects found in Siberia, among other things some pure gold diadems and bracelets dating from a very ancient civilisation (Scythian), also a headpiece made like chain mail from a lot of little silver pieces pierced and strung together. Among the curiosities concerning Peter I, M. Uvarov showed us a bound copybook in which the Tsar had drawn a sketch map during his stay in Holland, so as to explain a battle better to his host. The book had been preserved in this man's family until the Emperor Alexander visited Holland, when the owner offered it to him by way of homage.

In the evening I went to the theatre with Mlles Glasenapp and Tomatis, and we got back at ten o'clock when it was still light enough to read the time on my watch. I found Mlles Hogguer with Mama and Pauline. They are not very fond of their adopted countrymen and told us several anecdotes about them. Among other tales there is said to be a Central Russian magnate who has formed a troop of actresses among his serf girls, to a number of 300, and keeps them shut up in a prison tower, which they can only leave to act before him. Then there is another, either in Moscow or St Petersburg, who told his porter to send a certain person packing if he should present himself for dinner. This person met the gentleman by accident and complained. The consequence was the gentleman took him home with many apologies, asked him to stay to dinner, and during the meal treated him to the howls of the poor porter, who was being cruelly flogged for having carried out his master's orders. I was not a little surprised to be told that M. Pashkov, Count

Modène's son-in-law and colonel in the Guards Hussars, and his general, M. Levashov, both of whom have mild and pleasing faces, are so cruel to their subordinates. They are said to have breakfasted in comfort, while a wretched sergeant was flogged before their eyes for having obeyed his colonel's orders and thus disobeyed his general. The fact was that the colonel had incorrectly passed on the general's commands.

Friday, May 13th. We accompanied the Princess to the Bourse,[1] where the wind was so violent that we were nearly swept away under the portico. A deputation of merchants or perhaps the stewards of the building – Prince Cherbatov could not give us any information about them – met the Princess at the door and conducted her into the Great Hall, where the traders meet. It has a bust of Emperor Alexander, who had it built, and there are rooms all around it, which are used for sales. Some attics had been improvised under the roof to give shelter to people rendered homeless by the flood. The Exchange makes a very handsome impression at the angle of Vassil'evskii ostrov, all the more because of the two rostral columns acting as lighthouses at the point.

This was May 1st according to the Russian calendar, and is the day on which all St Petersburg goes to Catherinenhof, rather like the Parisians go to Longchamps. The court of Russia goes in state with footmen without overcoats whatever the weather, and mounted pages in light uniforms. The Dowager Empress was in an eight-horse coach and we followed in four-horse carriages. I was with Pauline, Mlle Kochetov and Prince Gagarin. All the carriages have to go in single file, private carriages on one side, droshkies on the other. As the court carriages drove separately from the others, we had the advantage of reviewing the whole world as it passed by. I did not see anything remarkable except for some fine horses, some troikas and teams of horses four abreast. There were

[1] Modelled after a Greek basilica at Paestum, the Bourse – the Commodity Exchange – was built in 1805-10 and designed by de Thomon. It is now the Central Naval Museum, containing exhibits which were housed in the Admiralty.

orchestras at intervals, as well as pleasure gardens, a restaurant and wooden towers with slides, but none of these were much frequented, though there was a crowd of people on foot. General Miloradovich, who had organised all of it, pranced round our carriages and assured us he felt very hot, although the wind would not allow us to have more than a single window open. There was not one leaf visible on any of the trees.

That evening we went to Mme Zagriazhskii's, where we had already met Count de Maistre several times, who is married to one of her nieces. I found out from her cousin, Countess Vorontsov, that he really is the author of *Voyage autour de ma chambre*. M. Saur [*sic*], the famous Spanish guitarist, was also at Mme Zagriazhskii's. He treated us again to 'The Little Beggar's Song', which I had already heard at Mme Naryshkin's.

The Prince is having a divine time in Moscow. He has sent the Princess violets from the Kremlin garden and a long list of parties, balls and spectacles they are arranging for him.

Sunday, May 15th. After church and duty at the Princess's audiences we dressed up without trains so as to be ready to go to the Smol'nyi convent, where a concert was to be given for the Dowager Empress by the girls of the community. Several of the young court ladies were among the party, having been educated there or in one of the other Institutes patronised by the Empress. We met in the Service Hall before setting out. I saw Princess Lise Volkonskii with her fiancé Prince Khilkov for the first time since their engagement was announced. Up to now he has always lived quietly, but has just accecpted a position as secretary to the Empress, which ties him completely to the court.

When we reached the convent we found all the noble and middle-class divisions drawn up in the refectory, the smallest in front, the larger girls behind, so they could all see what was going on. Fourteen pianos arranged in a semi-circle made us quite wrongly apprehensive of a dreadful din. The Empress and her children sat on a row of chairs at the other end of the room, Mme Adlerberg just behind her, and we a little further back. Two young girls played piano solos, and then Princess Khovanskii sang. She had become Mme Mansurov and had also been educated at the Empress's expense. We had already heard her at Gatchina, but in my opinion she was completely surpassed by Mlle Comnène, a descendant of the Byzantine Emperors and also a pupil at the Institute, who charmed in every way. Next the fourteen pianos started. Each instrument was played by four hands, so that there were fifty-six in all, as well as several voices. They played together with great unity and precision. Finally the Empress ordered that fine grace they sing before meals, and expressed her pleasure several times. She looked so happy with all these young people around her. You might have taken her for a good mother in the middle of her numerous family.

Monday, May 16th. Through M. van Heeckeren we had received Mme Gur'ev's permission to see the glass and porcelain factories outside the city. Prince Dolgorukii provided us with a dirty old carriage with six horses and we set out in the company of Messrs van Heeckeren and Everard. We left the city near the Nevskii Convent by the road that follows the river, fine and broad here, and we passed a seminary nearby. Some cows were grazing or pretending to graze beside the road, but two trees with a touch of green on them were the only things we saw showing a tiny sign of spring. Several gentlemen wearing decorations received us at the factory, where a lot of workmen were busy round a furnace with a fire shining through small apertures. First we were shown the basic ingredients of which glass is made. Then we saw a decanter and some glasses made in less than no time, and some glass thermometers and a large glass bell. We moved on to another workshop where a steam-pump drove a number of polishing stones, and saw a column for the glass bed ordered by the Emperor for the Shah of Persia. The Shah had asked for one to furnish a pavilion in which he rests during the midday heat, where he already has a crystal fountain given him by the Emperor. Later on we had the pleasure of seeing the whole bed complete. It was most interesting to see mirrors cast. This is done in an enormous furnace with little holes in it, through which you see a blaze worthy of hell. It is surrounded by figures wearing wide-brimmed hats to protect their faces from a fire so powerful that most of them had their garments singed. We watched this frightening spectacle from afar, not daring to approach because of the heat. In another workshop they quicksilvered a little mirror before us. Then we saw vases, breakfast and dinner sets, bottles etc. A very pretty breakfast set, with four beautiful vases, was given us as a present from the factory. We thanked the gentlemen very much, and got into our carriage to go on to the porcelain works nearby.

Here we were again received by gentlemen wearing decorations. The director could only speak Russian but he accompanied us everywhere, while the others gave explanations to us in German or French. They showed us a two-storey kiln where plates were being fired. In another room full of stucco models ranged along the wall there were young people, and even children, studying drawing so as to become designers, and to train their eyes by copying vases, etc. Every modelled or fluted object, from tiny saucer to whole vase, is machine-turned with astonishing speed. A soft formless mass of paste becomes an attractive cup in less than no time. All the workmen are crown serfs given to the factory; their children learn to draw and paint, and thus provide the necessary artists. The two best children had made beautiful works of art, though they are still a long way from the perfection reached at Sèvres. We saw some rather fine plates made for Count Arakcheev. They gave us presents, Mama a breakfast set and a pretty inkstand, Pauline and myself two pretty vases and a cup each. We got back to dinner at the apartments enchanted by our visits and the politeness they had shown us.

Tuesday, May 17th. Mama and the Princess dined with the Empress and in the evening there was a concert in the Service Hall, followed by supper in the Gatchina manner, that is at small tables for all who could not find a place at the big table, which had been lengthened like a comet, i.e. with a tail. The concert was charming thanks to the talent of the Romberg family, especially the father who plays the 'cello astonishingly well. His very young son tried his best to emulate his father, and his daughter sang but has not got a pleasant style. M. Saur [*sic*], the Spaniard, whom we had already heard on the guitar, surpassed himself that evening. He did not sing but played some most attractive pieces, among others a delightful march, which he was asked to repeat during dinner.

Thursday, May 19th. Ascension Day. It was very cold. After going to the Dutch church we had to put on trains to visit the Grand Duchess Elena, who received the court and town according to the custom of Grand Duchesses after their confinements.

Friday, May 20th. Rain and wind prevented our going walking in the morning. I drove out with Mama and paid calls in the evening after having received M. Zhukovskii. Talking of our imminent departure for the country he compared these stays in company with Their Highnesses to very beautiful landscapes one cannot enjoy because of wasps. Being a poet he could allow himself this bit of licence.

Saturday, May 21st. There was snow which did not make the weather milder. At dinner we did not forget to drink the health of Prince Frederick on the occasion of his marriage.

Sunday, May 22nd. We went to the Lutheran church to hear M. Reinbaud. I paid calls in the evening and on returning found the eldest Mlle Hogguer. They have plenty of sensational stories to tell which are extraordinary. A dweller in a distant quarter, she said, heard a noise in the night. He got up and saw the hand of a man trying to break the lock after making a hole in the door. The master of the house seized hold of the hand, sent his son out by another door to fetch the police, and waited patiently for his return without letting go. The police arrived, but imagine their amazement when they found a headless corpse. The other thieves saw their companion trapped, feared that he would give them away, so cut off his head without further ado and removed it to prevent all recognition. A second story concerns the death of a colonel, murdered like the captain a short time ago, an incident they take trouble to conceal. Finally an undoubtedly true and very unhappy tale, of the suicide of Count Laval's only son, who killed himself in Moscow after losing a huge sum at play.

Monday, May 23rd. All three of us drove to the Fortress. The Summer Garden bridge had not yet been restored, so we went by way of Vassil'evskii ostrov which is a long detour. We drove along the border of a vast expanse of grass where they were drying flax and hemp. It did not look like the outskirts of a great city. We passed three funerals on the way, afterwards entered the Fortress by a gate and drawbridge and stopped at the cathedral in the centre. It is the burial place for Russian sovereigns only. Instead of being buried in vaults their coffins stand in stone tombs at floor level, covered with richly embroidered stuffs under black palls, on which the name of the tomb's occupant is written in white letters. The church is decorated with an infinity of banners, Persian, Turkish, French and Polish, and the keys of various cities, but as all this was explained to us in Russian, we understood nothing or very little of the explanations.[2]

On our return I took a few turns in the Hermitage garden and at last saw a hint of green. The elder tree was beginning to show some leaves. That evening we visited Mme Cherbatov and Mme Naryshkin. The former was talking about spring being so late and assured us this year was exceptional and as a rule the month of May in St Petersburg is charming. She asked M. Palmstierna, the Swedish minister, to bear witness to her statement. 'I can assure you', he replied, 'I have spent several years in St Petersburg and I have never known a month of May to differ from this one.' We laughed a lot at Princess Cherbatov's disappointment when she got this answer. M. de Fontenay of the French embassy was also there and told us his

[2] The SS. Peter and Paul Fortress was founded by Peter the Great in 1703 and most of the buildings constructed in the following half century. The Cathedral was built by Trezzini and finished in 1733. All the Emperors and Empresses, except three, including Nicholas II, are buried there.

ambassador, Count de la Ferronaye, wanted to give a ball on the 29th for his King's coronation and that we were to be invited. Unfortunately our departure for Pavlovsk had been fixed for the 28th. However the news of the ball reached the ears of the Imperial family when the Grand Dukes and Princes had been invited, and the Princesses thought it right to leave part of their retinues in town out of politeness to the ambassador. The Prince of Orange delegated me for this purpose with Pauline and M. Wauthier.

Tuesday, May 24th. The warmth of the sun contrasted disagreeably with a very cold wind and the combination of the two upset us a good deal. The fruits of all kinds the Princess was receiving from the Emperor's hothouses contrasted with the bitterness of the season. One day she gave us apricots. M. Wauthier came back from Moscow enchanted by the city and made us long to go there. The populace had crowded round the Prince, filling the air with their hurrahs, so much so that M. Wauthier had thought himself in Amsterdam.

Saturday, May 28th. The day of the Imperial family's departure. I went with Mama to look at Peter the Great's little house, the first he occupied in what was then an uninhabited wilderness. It is on the bank of the river opposite the Summer Garden. Thanks to the bridge of boats which had just been replaced we were able to go straight there and at the same time enjoy a splendid view of the river. The bridge of boats crosses it at what is nearly its widest point. A quantity of busy little craft and one big steamship enlivened the Neva, while the fine buildings on the banks, seen altogether from the middle of the bridge, struck us all the more because it seemed like saying goodbye to this beautiful city, which we would probably never see again except for a few moments. Peter's little house is incredibly small. In order to preserve it better it has been enclosed under a wooden hangar, open at the sides, together with a little boat the Tsar built with his own hands.[3]

[3] Peter lived in this small cabin from 1703 to 1709. The boat is today in the Central Naval Museum.

At five o'clock we bade farewell to the Princess and Mama, who left for Pavlovsk where we were to follow them two days later. I spent another hour in my room, after which I went with Pauline to visit the Modènes, Grand Duke Nicholas's French controller and his wife, whom we found walking in the Anichkov Palace garden, where the greenery was really beginning to show. Mme de Modène showed us her husband's very handsome apartment and invited us to go with her to see the play in the little theatre next to the Anichkov Palace. The play itself was boring but the Modènes' box was very much more confortable than the Imperial one. One of the French attachés came to tell us that the ambassador was very unwell, which for a short time made us fear the ball might be put off.

Sunday, May 29th. Russian Pentecost. We went to our respective churches and then after dinner got into a modest cab to drive to Catherinenhof where it is customary to go on May 1st. There were many more people than on the 1st, and the line of carriages began inside the city. It was not long before we found that it is a very different thing to go there in the Empress's suite from going in an ordinary cab. Everyone passed us and our old screws hardly managed to move. Twenty times I would have liked to turn back but controlled myself out of consideration for my friend, who afterwards said she had felt the same.

We got back to the apartment about eight, dressed for the ball and went there about ten with Countesses Fritsch and Tomatis. It was still bright daylight. The ambassador was present but poorly, all the embassy gentlemen very polite, and Countess Ludolf, the wife of the minister of Naples, was doing the honours. All the apartments were decorated with lovely lilies. The Grand Duke Michael and the Prince of Saxe-Weimar came for a few moments, the Grand Duke only spoke to men, and both men departed before supper. I should have liked to do the same but we had been told that, as we represented the court, it was essential that we stay for supper, especially as they were to drink the health of the new King of

France, something they did not in fact do. Supper was served in a fine room, all decorated with flowers, and with an orchestra in the balcony playing very attractive music. The principal table in the middle was covered with gold plate, and every lady had a bouquet on her napkin. As soon as it was over we departed. It was three o'clock and the sun was beginning to rise. I got to bed at four, to get up again at eight and leave with Pauline at ten for Pavlovsk.

We travelled in an excellent carriage from the Imperial stables. There was still only a little greenery here and there. We reached the palace of Pavlovsk by a back door, very close to our apartment on the first floor. Mama's rooms and mine looked out onto the front, Pauline's the back. Just opposite us is a guard room where the band of a Hussar regiment comes to play each evening between seven and nine. They end every day by playing the grace sung in all the Institutes, and the guard listens under arms with caps off. It is a very solemn and moving spectacle and was one of my greatest pleasures when I managed to be in my room at nine, a pleasure I did not often enjoy. I did not find Mama when I arrived in our apartment. She was in the Lutheran church at Tsarskoe with one of the Saxe-Weimar princesses who had just arrived.

We were sent for by the Princess who has a delicious apartment on the ground floor. It belongs to her mother, who wants to spare her the fatigue of climbing stairs and has herself moved one floor higher. She received us in a charming salon, furnished in grey satinwood and hung with hangings embroidered in the Institutes. A door with gauze-protected windows to keep out the midges leads into a garden full of all the flowers the climate permits, cultivated with the greatest care. There is an arbour and, by way of curiosities, a pear tree and a chestnut which they cover up in winter, as well as some fine clumps of lilies which were very far from being in flower. A boudoir next to the salon has some precious pictures. The whole apartment is a jewel. The Princess showed us round and told us that evening we must put on ball dresses for the celebration of the marriage of Prince Khilkov to Princess Volkonskii. Marriage is epidemic here as this is a marriage market for the maids of honour.

I found Mama when we got back to our rooms, and we were forced to have a fire lit for the first days of our stay. Our rooms were very cold. Mama dined with the Empress; we were at the Marshal's table where we found all the Gatchina ladies with the exception of the Michael court. The company was joined by General Prince Khilkov, elder brother of the bridegroom of the day. Three rooms were used before, during and after dinner, a dining room, a billiard room with pictures painted by the Princess, and a salon full of flowers, communicating with the garden by three French windows and a flight of steps. There is a very pretty view over a piece of water, a cascade and a small temple, and beyond a prospect of the church of Pavlovsk and the fortress where the pages lodge.

At eight we gathered for the wedding in a gallery next door to the Empress's apartments. The bride soon emerged, conducted by the Grand Duke Michael, called the 'seated father', and the Grand Duchess Maria 'the seated mother'. I do not fully understand the meaning of these titles, they seem to mean no more than leading bride and groom to the church and being placed close to them. Prince Khilkov had two of his near relations for this purpose. According to custom he was waiting for her in the chapel. She wore a tulle dress, ornamented with bouquets of orange flowers, and on her head all the diamonds the Dowager Empress could manage to arrange there. She always presides over the dressing of her maids of honour when they are married, and covers them with diamonds kept for these occasions. The bride takes off her gloves and gives them with her handkerchief to her 'seated mother'. The Empress enters and the ceremony begins.

Apart from several long exhortations and prayers of which I understood nothing, I noticed that a piece of pink satin was laid before the couple, onto which they had to step together. They say the spouse who is the first to step on it will rule the household. Then they are made to drink some sour wine from the same cup to signify that all misfortunes must be shared in marriage. Finally their hands are joined, the priest covers them with a fold of his vestment and, holding them together, leads them three times round the altar. The ceremony being finished the couple approached the Empress and kissed her hand to thank her, then everyone embraced them, and we went into a salon for a little ball. (I have omitted one of the ceremonies, which is extremely tiring for the people concerned. During part of the service two young people, both unmarried but related to the couple, have to hold a crown over the couple's heads.) At the ball the polonaises lasted a long time. The groom was expected to dance with each of the Princesses and First Ladies, and the bride with all the Princes and most of the men. In fact she did not dance at all, as her head-dress was too heavy. She spent most of the evening between the Empress and the Grand Duchess Maria.

Tuesday, May 31st. I began the day with a long walk with Mama and Mlle Kochetov, while Pauline was with the Princess. First we called on the Nelidov ladies in their little wooden house, built by the Emperor for the aunt. The wooden Alexander Pavilion, inhabited by the Grand Duke Nicholas and his wife when they are at Pavlovsk, is next door. A little further on we followed a path across a lawn with a little clump of trees, and saw across a small pond a very pretty house inhabited by Princess Gagarin and her family. You get there by a little ferry. The Princess was not at home, so we went on walking to the Constantine Pavilion, which is close by. We called on Countess El'mpt, who has a very small apartment there. We found the newly married couple there, paying the customary round of calls. When we left, Mlle Kochetov, who is a good walker and has little pity on our legs, took us first to the Rose Pavilion, where we later had many enjoyable parties, then to the Peace Pavilion and finally the farm, where there is an attractive balcony room with books and ink and paper, used by people to record their visits, quite a drawerful of them. As for ourselves, cream and good bread and butter pleased us better than the idea of writing witty tributes after a long walk. When we had recovered our strength a little they showed us over the cow house in full detail. The farm is looked after by Germans, and the milk is kept in a dairy cooled with ice which keeps the temperature extremely cold.

That day the Dowager Empress dined on the ground floor with all of us, and in the evening we assembled in the salon to listen to some reading. Candles were lit despite the light of day and a row of little games tables set up around the principal table as they were at Gatchina. Hardly had a few pages of M. de Ségur's book been read,[4] when a letter arrived for the Empress from the Grand Duchess Alexandrine. They had long been arguing where she was to lie in. The Grand Duke wanted to remain in St Petersburg, but the Anichkov Palace is not habitable during the great summer heat. The Grand Duchess did not want to come to Pavlovsk, where the Empress wanted her, preferring to stay at Tsarskoe Selo. As the doctors had been told to say the palace at Pavlovsk was too damp, the letter which had just arrived could announce her wish to come to Pavlovsk. The Empress at once withdrew to answer it – and refuse in view of the opinion of the doctors. Thus it was settled that the Grand Duchess Alexandrine would occupy the Alexander Palace at Tsarskoe Selo.

Pauline complained of pains which had got much worse during the night, and in the following days she was in real danger.

June

Wednesday, June 1st. Mama dined downstairs with me but stayed with our invalid during the evening, while I went to the salon where the reading was continued for adults, and the

---

[4] Presumably Philippe de Ségur's *Histoire de Napoléon et de la Grande Armée*, which had been published with great success in 1824.

younger ladies were put in an adjoining room to play games with the Saxe-Weimar princesses. The Prince of Saxe-Weimar came to join us and took an enthusiastic part in recreations fit for children of eight to ten years old, while at the same time telling us a mass of anecdotes, some true, some false, all boring.

Thursday, June 2nd. Our friend was bad, and I accompanied the Princess to the service, after which the Empress received the congratulations of the whole court on the Saints' day of Sts Helen and Constantine. The Princess was extremely worried about our invalid, as we were too, and called at the Grand Duke Michael's door to tell him that if we got still more concerned she would not come to the family dinner he was giving in honour of his wife, Grand Duchess Elena. He followed us to ask details of Pauline's condition with real sympathy. The Princess let herself be dissuaded from dining at home, which would have done no good.

Friday, June 3rd. The invalid continued getting worse, but the Dowager Empress kept appearing in the salon and assuring me that she was better. Her doctor, who had been called in consultation, had told her so. At the same time she was full of attention for the poor sick lady and came several times a day to ask about her without entering her room, so as not to disturb her. She saw to it that she should want for nothing.

Saturday, June 4th. Pauline was a little better, and Mama dined downstairs while I was upstairs with the doctor, to be within reach. Outings with the Princess almost always fell to me during these days, and on one of them she took me to her father's monument. It is a square building with a columned peristyle and marble walls. Inside there is a mausoleum surrounded by statues of the Empress and her children. The Dowager Empress has put up monuments in her garden to many dead relations, children, parents, husband. When I came back from these excursions I relieved Mama beside our friend so that she could take a little air.

Sunday, June 5th. The invalid was in a very alarming state again. I went to service with the Princess and dined downstairs in the ordinary salon, because there were few guests. Messrs Buturlin and Divov were opposite me at table and Mlle Sylvestre was next to me, so that our conversation was very animated. At seven we met again after changing our dresses and putting on veils and cloaks to guard against the dust in the *lineika* carriages, which were to take us to the Rose Pavilion. These *lineiki* are like double settees on very low wheels drawn by six horses. You sit back to back, three or four people on each side, seeing neither your neighbours nor the road you are driving on. You are much suffocated by the dust and by the veil and cloak you have to wrap yourself in very tight. Once we had got to the end of our drive we shook ourselves, folded our cloaks and entered the Pavilion. It consists of three or four small rooms and a large hall, which was added when the Emperor returned from the war. It is still hung with garlands of roses and laurels, which the Institutes made for the feast the Empress gave for her son.[1] The Pavilion was surrounded by a crowd of curious people pressing against the windows. There was a balcony where the Empress amused herself for some time by watching little girls and ladies sliding down the wooden slides she had built for them. There was even a swing for people who like it. When we went inside there were some gentlemen standing in a corner and the ladies, lacking partners, danced with one another, which was rather like a dancing class. We supped at little tables, and at ten o'clock carriages drove us home. 'The cousins were given supper; they are unbearable.'[2]

Monday, June 6th. The weather had at last turned mild and I was quite surprised, on waking up, to see the lime trees, which up till then had only shown imperceptible buds, covered with leaves in a single night. In less than two days the change was complete and we found ourselves in midsummer without having had any spring. It became very hot, and I was walking with Mlle Sylvestre at half past eight in the morning. Our

[1] This was on 27 July/8 August 1814 when Alexander paid a short visit to his capital before the Congress of Vienna.
[2] Cornélie is presumably referring to the Württembergs.

invalid was slightly better, which allowed Mama to go out with the Princess and to dine with me downstairs. About midday the heat was stifling and I paid a call with Countess Fritsch on the newly married Khilkov couple, who have been established for some days in Pavlovsk, a place which hardly merits being called a town. All the houses are wooden with very modest exteriors and built lightly as if for an Italian climate. Inside they are tastefully furnished and serve as country perches for a good many courtiers during the summer. Princess Khilkov's house is particularly tiny but she is very happy and contented there. Mama joined in the excursion and supper that evening, and I stayed with my friend who was at last out of danger.

Tuesday, June 7th. I walked with Countess Fritsch who showed me the monument to the Empress's parents.

Wednesday, June 8th. A vain alarm about the Grand Duchess Alexandrine sent the Empress to Tsarskoe. She came back after dinner for a few hours only and returned there in the evening to stay until her daughter-in-law's confinement, taking Princess Khilkov and M. Villamov, not to mention the good doctor Ruhle. The evening was enchanting and we heard a nightingale in the garden, so great a wonder in this neighbourhood that Mlle Kochetov stopped the carriage so as to hear it more clearly.

Thursday, June 9th. The Grand Duchess Maria and her sister dined with us, and that evening we met again so as to await the Dowager Empress, who was coming specially from Tsarskoe to take her daughters for a little snack in the new chalet, after first inspecting some rose trees and other shrubs she had planted in pots between the aviary and the theatre. We sat down at a line of tables in a chalet where you can hardly turn round, and the Empress handed fruit and cream to everyone. When she had finished she got back in her carriage and drove back to Tsarskoe. We walked back to the palace on a very lovely night, admiring the lilies which were all in flower.

Friday, June 10th. A pear tree and a small chestnut flowered in the Princess's garden, and I took a morning walk with her in the two 'sylvies', the name they give to two small spinneys filled with bowers and statues in the French style, the only places giving any shade close to the palace. We dined at the Marshal's table. Their Highnesses were at Tsarskoe and we were to go there immediately after dinner to share a picnic the reigning Empress was giving at her dairy farm. She had been kind enough to ask the Grand Duchesses to bring all their ladies with them, so that we could have the pleasure of seeing her beautiful farm at Tsarskoe. Mama was with the Princess and I arranged to go with Mlle Sylvestre in a droshky. We left at the same time as the Grand Duchess Maria but unfortunately our coachman took the canal route, whereas the others followed the main road. At first we were delighted to avoid the dust and bumping of the *chausée*, but when we got to Tsarskoe we had lost Their Highnesses' trail and did not know where to go. We looked for help from Mlle Glasenapp but she was not at home. I wanted to go and see the Empress's two other ladies but it was useless.

So we were forced to give up and, to pass the time, my friend suggested that we go and look at the Colonnade. We left the palace by a service door. It is an enormous building, sixty-four windows broad without counting the wings, which lengthen the façade. There is a big forecourt, edged with minor buildings and apartments for the gentlemen. Behind the palace there are lovely lime trees casting a refreshing shade. The whole garden is kept up with extraordinary care, the lawns are splendid and the paths so well looked after that you hardly pass before a little workman appears to remove your traces. The Emperor likes to be able to walk in his park as if he were in his salon, without a speck of dust on his shoes. Eight hundred to a thousand men are constantly kept busy keeping up this ravishing retreat, with instructions to stay out of sight of walkers whenever possible, so that the whole place seems like fairyland.

The Colonnade we were about to see consists of a charming gallery leading from a little garden to some apartments separate from the palace, which the Empress Catherine had had built. This garden lies above a vault on the first-floor level which you reach by driving up an incline. There are antique bronze busts on either side and you have a delightful views towards a pretty lake, on which floats a small ship, apparently fully loaded, which has remained there since the Grand Duchess Catherine, Queen of Württemberg, cruised in it on her last visit to Tsarskoe.[3] After the garden the Colonnade ends with a splendid double staircase flanked by colossal statues. We visited the Empress Catherine's apartment, a suite of only three or four rooms where she used to stay during the heat of summer. The walls are lined with marble and porphyry, the ceilings painted and the parquets exquisitely polished.

We then went back to Mlle Glasenapp's, who at last came home but knew nothing whatever about the picnic. She had only just begun her duty with the reigning Empress and her fellow ladies were rather cold-shouldering her. We learned that Mama and Countess El'mpt had driven up to look for us during our excursion to the Colonnade, but, having failed to find us, had driven off again. So we decided to give up the notion of going to the farm for fear of having to make an embarrassing entrance, and merely set out walking in the park with Mlle Glasenapp. I was astonished by the beautiful vegetation in comparison with Pavlovsk. I must say that at Tsarskoe you really forget you are in Russia. The lakes look beautiful and the fountains never stop running, whereas at Pavlovsk you find a pensioner standing sentinel over the smallest trickle. He only turns it on when he observes a carriage or some people of distinction approaching. We passed a spring which had been cleverly used to represent the fable of the milkmaid and the broken milk pot.

[3] This was the Emperor Alexander's favourite sister, who was born in 1788 and died in 1819. The Colonnade was the Cameron Gallery, built in 1783-6 and regarded as one of Charles Cameron's masterpieces. It is now used for exhibitions. The palaces and town of Tsarskoe Selo were destroyed by the Germans in the Second World War, since when the buildings have been repaired and restoration continues.

The maid is on her knees on a block of granite and the water pours out of the broken pot in front of her. After this we came into an avenue of oaks, really quite fine for Russia and tended by the Emperor with the greatest care.

We had just entered it when we saw a line of droshkies approaching. The Empress Elizabeth and the Grand Duchess Maria were in the first. The Empress stopped her carriage and asked what had hindered us from coming with the other ladies, who had been told to bring us to the farm. My two companions being tongue-tied, I explained to Her Majesty that we had had bad luck in missing her messengers, and so had simply taken a walk. The Empress pressed us to come to the rendezvous notwithstanding, provided we felt strong enough, and asked Mlle Glasenapp if she knew the way sufficiently well to take us there. She replied that she did, and so the Empress drove off, followed by her suite including the Grand Duchess Elena and the Princesses of Orange, Württemberg and Saxe-Weimar, all of whom had been kept waiting.

We had still plenty of walking to do without being too sure of our way. First we passed the Chinese village, so called for its chinoiserie buildings which serve as country houses for several St Petersburg personalities more or less connected with the court. Countess Ozarovskii, the aide-de-camp's wife, is one of them; as we passed her house, she showed us how to find our way. We passed a theatre, used for parties in the time of Catherine, the Alexander Palace, a fine building with a colonnade, then a pretty artificial ruin and at last we saw the farm. We then met the Dowager Empress driving homewards in an open carriage with the Grand Duchess Alexandrine, which made me think Their Highnesses had left. However, seeing several ladies at a window, we thought this must be the suite awaiting us. Full of this idea we went up to the door, which was opened for us by the Empress Elizabeth herself. She then opened another door into a room containing all the ladies of the court and led us in, remarking 'I bring you some lost sheep.' Her Majesty then rejoined the Imperial family and we did honour to the refreshments, fruit and dairy produce and some excellent waffles.

Then on to the cow-house, where we found the whole Imperial family. They were having black bread handed to them on plates and giving it to the cows. I had never been in a cow-house in such high society, but of course it is not like any other cow-house. It is a large cruciform room with a waxed floor and a partition separating you from the animals, so high that you can only see them if you stand on tiptoe. The cows stand on planks and are separated from each other by low barriers. They eat from mangers built against the main partition with the name of every animal written up. The Emperor has taken pleasure in collecting beasts from every country. I found some countrywomen, including *Lekenvelder*. There are Swiss and Tyrolean cows and Hungarians with enormous horns. Each herd grazes separately in the fields round Tsarskoe, being taken out in the morning and brought back every night. People of different nations look after the animals in the dairy, with an English woman in overall charge. You descend a double spiral staircase, as if in a tower, with milk in pots like ours standing in ice along the walls. Nothing could be cleaner. When they are milking even the milk pails stand in little tents to stop the slightest dust from getting in the milk. They groom the cows like horses. The reigning Empress did the honours of her farm with charm and forgot none of us. Her figure seems a little better than last autumn but she is still weak and her complexion is as ghastly as ever. She asked both me and Mama more than once if my walk had not been bad for me, and was kind enough to write next day for news of me through Mlle Glasenapp. About ten o'clock I drove back to Pavlovsk with the Princess of Orange, Prince Augustus of Saxe-Weimar and Mlle Sylvestre.

'In three months' time [Cornélie wrote home] I hope to be in Brussels, but I must admit the idea of four weeks' driving in this heat, half of it on horrible sand tracks, terrifies me for an invalid like Pauline. As for me I would brave the deserts of Arabia to be back with you.'

Saturday, June 11th. We dined at the Marshal's table, after which I followed the example of other ladies and picked a few flowers in the drawing room. This is something not permitted by the Dowager Empress, and Prince Dolgorukii, the Grand Duchess Maria's Chamberlain, called me a republican or a constitutionalist. He told me that he himself was an obedient slave and would never do such a thing. That evening I accompanied the Princess to the Grand Duchess Elena's, where she stayed a long time. I spent it walking with the maids of honour and then at Countess El'mpt's, where we could observe the deference which which the servants spoke to Vasili, the Emperor's coachman, a fat man with a long beard who always drives the Princess.

Sunday, June 12th. The weather, which had been very hot for eight days, changed to wind and rain with very cold evenings. We dined twice over the next few days with the Dowager Empress, the Grand Duchesses and the Prince of Saxe-Weimar. The Princess of Orange did not wait for her sister to appear with her as usual but made haste to arrive first and do the honours. There were a couple of other occasions when the Grand Duchess Maria made us spend an evening playing childish games, another playing lotto.

Tuesday, June 14th. In the evening Mlle Kochetov took us with Countess Fritsch along a very bad road to a village called Fedorovskoe, a fairly pretty place for a Russian village. The church, school and priest's house are quite attractive. A cavalcade of several ladies went with us, each with a squire for company, among whom was Prince Trubetskoi, the fiancé of the younger Nelidov. At Fedorovskoe we got out at the village headman's, who was not at home. His wife and mother received us most politely and took us up to the first floor of their solid wooden house. We found a large room with benches along the walls and a stove, round which were gathered all the women of the family. They look after their figures so badly that their belts are fastened above their breasts. The headman's wife however had a pretty face. She showed us their main living room with the baby's cradle hung up in the middle and beds, I think, behind screens. The peasants always sleep on matting or on the stoves. They gave us sour rye bread with cream and curds, after which we drove home. The country is ugly, with a few fields round the village of poor rye that had only been in ear for the last week, and otherwise nothing but swamp and scrub.

Thursday, June 16th. After having visited Mme Pleshcheev in her attractive country house, we spent the evening with Prince Gagarin in an even more delightful place. Mlle Nelidov danced the shawl dance, to her future husband's delight. He had never seen her do it before and 'was so enchanted that he had no eyes or ears for anything else around him'. The two of them make a charming couple.

Sunday, June 19th. The Dowager Empress came to dine and as there were a lot of people we used the square room next to our apartment. Before dinner we met in a gallery leading to the Empress's rooms, and after in the Greek Hall, a fine colonnaded room just above our salon. There was a dance that evening in the lower salon because the rain was pouring down, which made the Rose Pavilion impossible. More Tsarskoe people came to these dances than to those in St Petersburg. I danced twelve polonaises that evening as there were plenty of partners – which is rare.

Monday, June 20th. We were able to drive in a *lineika* after dinner to see the German colonists near Tsarskoe. These are the latest arrivals, though there are others who have been in the neighbourhood for eighty years and preserved their faith and language. They have many privileges, their houses have been built at government expense and are very good, they are given land to clear, and only begin paying taxes after ten years. They have set up a workshop to make stay-laces and cotton ribbons, and their gardens are cultivated with a tidiness and care which in themselves show they are not Russians. The ones we visited came from the Rhineland, but when we asked one if he missed his country, he replied 'One's country is wherever one can eat.' His wife however did recall her homeland's vines and fruits with pleasure. We went on to the Tsarskoe fair, a little row of stalls with lotteries and games of roulette.

Wednesday, June 22nd. Pauline took a bath that evening in my presence. Her convalescence has been very slow. The Prince of Orange came back from Warsaw the next day and was struck by her emaciation. The family dined alone together but appeared that evening. We had to play at various very tiring games like blind-man's buff, the war game, forfeits and some others whose names I have forgotten.

Friday, June 24th. Mama told me of a plan which terrified me. She thought Pauline would not be well enough to travel with the Princess or ahead of her, and wanted me to accompany the Princess, while she would follow with Pauline. I took a solitary walk to try to swallow this gloomy proposition. The next day I tried again to argue against it, but in vain; and so resigned myself. On that day the Grand Duchess Alexandrine gave birth to a daughter. In the evening I drove with the Gagarins and Dolgorukiis to Bablovo, a hunting lodge a little beyond Tsarskoe. Princess Dolgorukii, who was with me in the droshky, explained the etymology of the name of Tsarskoe. When Catherine I, the wife of Peter the Great, began the palace she liked the place because it was near a peasant woman friend of hers called Sara; so she named the palace and village 'Sarskoe Selo' or 'Sara's village'. Later they changed the name to 'Tsarskoe Selo' which means 'Tsar's village'. The Princess also pointed out the granite pyramid in the middle of the lake, commemorating the naval victory of Chesma won by Alexis Orlov against the Turks [in 1770]. For this victory he was given the added name Chesmenskii, and was the father of the lady-in-waiting whom we knew.

Sunday, June 26th. They sang a Te Deum for the newly born Grand Duchess Alexandra Nikolaevna, but the court was given leave not to attend and so we went to our own church at Pavlovsk. Dinner was at the Marshal's table, and that evening

I drove with Mlle Lunin to Tsarskoe Selo to call on Princess Khilkov and Mlle Glasenapp. The latter was in waiting and was very soon summoned to the Empress Elizabeth. Princess Khilkov also had to go out with the Dowager Empress but saw us on the landing and asked us to wait in her room. We climbed a lot of stairs and spent nearly an hour in her tiny apartment with a very wide view of the country from above one of the palace wings.

As Princess Khilkov did not come back we set out for Pavlovsk, but as we drove along the terrace behind the palace our lucky star brought us up against the Emperor himself, setting out in his solitary droshky. A servant rode in front of him with his greatcoat. My companion was enchanted and squeezed my arm with pleasure. We stopped to let His Majesty pass, but he got out and came to ask for news of Pauline. He asked me if I liked the country, and when I said yes, added I was spoilt by the enchanting neighbourhood of Brussels. They never talk of our fine beauties in the northern Netherlands, and the most that could be said of hereabouts was that it was green. I answered with a speech in praise of Tsarskoe and its fine trees, whereupon the Emperor said it might perhaps remind me a little of the Netherlands. He also said a few words to Mlle Lunin and left us, having asked me to present his compliments to Mama. We watched him dash off in his droshky, which had been waiting for him behind a lilac bush. I spent the rest of the evening with Pauline, who is beginning to recover a little strength.

Monday, June 27th. After dinner we took a rather attractive drive with a large company in a *lineika* and some droshkies. Prince Gagarin had ordered tea to be ready in a nearby German village, but when we got there it had not arrived. So we got out of our carriages and crossed the village on foot.

All the children were talking German, which they teach before Russian. We followed the path through cornfields till we reached another German village where tea arrived at last, having lost its way and been upset en route, and a very pretty picnic set belonging to the Prince had been damaged. We had soon organised a nice picnic on the lawn below the church, where a village woman brought us butter and plenty of milk. The Russians are terribly extravagant with milk. Our party merely removed the cream and left the rest in the pots on the ground as if their contents were worth nothing more.

July

Friday, July 1st. There was to be a great review in St Petersburg on the 2nd in honour of the Prince of Orange. Although the Emperor had invited his sisters to stay at Kamennyi ostrov, where there is little room, without their suites, His Majesty thought the foreign courts should also be represented. As Pauline did not accept my offer to stay with her, I left with Mama and our maids at noon for the city. We found the Winter Palace shrouded in gloom though the Hermitage garden was full of orange blossom, green and pretty. There were a thousand doubts about next day, since it had started raining and no one knew if there was to be a parade and, if so, when. Contradictory news arrived continually, but the latest message told us we were to be ready before seven o'clock.

Saturday, July 2nd. The regimental bands marching along the Millionaya to the Champ de Mars awakened us before five. At half past six we met at Countess Fritsch's with Messrs Bielke and Vitzthum and Princes Dolgorukii and Cherbatov. Two landaus were ready for us, and an equerry was ordered to inform us when the Emperor left Kamennyi ostrov. We got into our carriages and waited near the Marble Palace for the Imperial cortège, which soon crossed the Summer Garden bridge. The Emperor and the Prince of Orange mounted their horses and we followed the Grand Duchesses. Their carriages halted by the Champ de Mars facing the infantry, with the cavalry and artillery behind them. I was a little frightened when I noticed three or four wagons rather like bathing-machines drawn up along-side, and was told they were to remove the sick and wounded. As soon as the Emperor appeared on the Champ de Mars the bands of all the regiments struck up together in perfect unison, a general cheer rose everywhere and was repeated by each regiment as he rode past the ranks.

These 40,000 men, composed of the élite of Russia's troops, made a magnificent spectacle. The music played included 'God Preserve Our Tsar' and a good deal from *Freischütz*. Once he had ridden round the ranks the Emperor took up his position near the carriage which contained his sisters and nieces, with the Prince of Saxe-Weimar a little to the rear beside the generals in the Emperor's suite. His Majesty wore the ribbon of King William's military order and sent all reports that reached him to the Prince of Orange, who was in command. The infantry marched past with the Grand Dukes Nicholas and Michael at the head of their divisions, taking their places afterwards behind the Emperor, like the other general officers.

The Grand Duke Michael's division went by first. Among its regiments they pointed out the Emperor Paul's Grenadiers, one of the bravest units in the recent war. By way of recompense for its conduct it has kept the mitred headgear which the whole Russian army used to wear. These helmets have copper plates in front, about which the French used to say 'Let's aim at the bronze', and some of them still show bullet-holes. They are kept like treasures in the regiment and it is an honour to wear them. General Miloradovich was riding up and down, and sometimes came to talk to us. He told us that during the French war this very regiment, knowing it was his name-day, paid him special honours. He had answered 'Lads, I have no money on me, but over there is a column of Frenchmen, and I give them to you.' Nothing more was needed to destroy those luckless French, and the Pavlovskiis let only two men escape. They attacked the enemy without firing, simply with their bayonets fixed. Next came the Semenovskii regiment, which was broken up some years ago for mutiny.[1] Then came the Preobrazhenskii, the first regiment of Foot Guards, followed by the Carabinier cadets, still very young, all orphan sons of soldiers. They are brought up at the Crown's expense and taught reading, writing and some geometry, so that later they can take commissions in the line. The farriers are not attached to the various regiments as in other armies, but form a separate corps with axes on their backs, to be distributed in time of war as needed. Police officers, stationed eight or ten paces apart, marked the straight line these soldiers had to follow. The first time they marched past in threes in slow and melancholy time. Their discipline was such that, all together, they seemed to form a single mechanism. Near us their lines appeared to bend a little, but everyone agreed that of its kind their bearing was unique.

After the infantry, the cavalry trotted past to an enchanting tune in the following order: Cavalier Guards, Horse Guards, the Emperor's Cuirassiers, the Dowager Empress's Cuirassier Regiment, Hussars, Lancers and finally Cossacks. Each regiment had its colour for its horses, the officers' horses being smaller, with docked tails. They look magnificent. Most of the troopers' horses are chestnuts or greys. Some of the senior officers, among them Count Orlov, have very valuable mounts. The Light Artillery followed with lovely teams fit to draw ceremonial coaches.

When all this was over the infantry and cavalry marched past a second time in battalion formation, followed by the Horse Artillery and the Pontoon Regiment under Grand Duke Michael. When the troops were back in line the Grand

[1] These words of Miloradovich are repeated in a similar anecdote by Tolstoi in *War and Peace* (vol. 4, part 4, ch. 4). They involve a different, cavalry, regiment. No casualties were inflicted and Tolstoi draws a totally different moral conclusion. The perforated helmets of the Pavlovskii regiment remained in honoured use until the Revolution. The Semenovskii, second, regiment of Foot Guards had refused to obey its commanding officer, Major-General Schwartz, because of his intolerable discipline. It had accepted wholesale arrest without resistance, but as revolutionary influence was suspected by Emperor Alexander it was disbanded. Schwartz was universally blamed and later brought to trial by court martial.

Dukes thanked them and the Emperor showed his satisfaction by giving the men a rouble each, as well as meat and vodka. We did not hear of any accidents except that one officer had fallen off his horse – so we were informed by Colonel Bibikov, the Grand Duke Michael's ADC. He himself had lost his plume, and later we were told that several soldiers had fainted from tight lacing.

Their Highnesses returned to Kamennyi ostrov and we to the Winter Palace. The weather was superb and the Neva in all its beauty. I went out on the balcony to watch the various regiments marching back to barracks and the detachments bringing flags back to the palace. The trumpets of the Cavalier Guards played their delightful march again. After we had dined with the Saxe-Weimar ladies and Countess Tomatis, I drove round the islands with Mama and Messrs Goblet and Everard. We crossed the Summer Garden and followed wooden duckboards which took us comfortably across the Apothecary's Island to Kamennyi ostrov. The palace stands on an island between two branches of the Neva. Quite soon we crossed a bridge and drove for several minutes on the coast towards Finland, but had to turn back for Elagin, another very pretty island with a palace.

On our way back to Pavlovsk in another carriage our postilion fell off his horse. The poor child screamed quite dreadfully and we could not even ask him where the pain was. Luckily the Grand Duchess Maria drove up and got us out of trouble. She had the child put in another carriage and driven off to Pavlovsk; he was all right in a few days. These poor little postilions have a wretched life and I think a lot of them die early. They are constantly exposed to every sort of weather and the accidents of their calling, and they are often only ten to twelve years old. At Pavlovsk we found our invalid getting on quite well. In the following week she tried some drives and walks, but the latter suited her better.

Saturday, July 9th. The Prince of Orange left with the Emperor for the military colonies.

Sunday, July 10th. We were free all day. After church we drove to Tsarskoe in the evening with some other people. We went in a *lineika* to the Park Gate with the triumphal arch, erected by the Emperor after the late wars, and inscribed 'To my dear companions in arms' in golden letters, in Russian and French on opposite sides. Then we walked round the very beautiful lake, where the syringas were beginning to flower. On our way we looked at several pavilions, one of which contains a lift for raising a large table, ready laid, to the first floor. None of this is now in use and some of the buidings are in ruins, but the lawns, trees and paths are all better cared for. We passed a monument surrounded with flat tombstones covered with inscriptions to the Empress Catherine's dogs. Last of all we climbed a tower built like a ruin and got a very fine view over the flat countryside.

Tuesday, July 12th. We dined under the colonnade where the sun was not too strong and there is a wooden floor. I drank to Agatha's health with all my neighbours.

Wednesday, July 13th. The Grand Duchess Alexandrine's name-day, and there was a great dinner upstairs followed by a ball in the Rose Pavilion. I never saw a chillier or more boring one, as there was not a single partner.

Thursday, July 14th. I went with the Princess in a landaulet to Tsarskoe, where she called on the Grand Duchess Alexandrine and I spent fifteen minutes waiting in an antechamber. Then we left for the new chalet, an attractive thatched cottage in the Pavlovsk wood with fountains round it. The Dowager Empress joined us with the whole court in *lineikas*, and we all got into these delightful carriages, where the dust nearly stifled us. The evening ended with a supper in the big room at the farm. These suppers are always the same, whatever corner of the earth you eat them in.

Friday, July 15th. In the evening we were all to go for a drive in landaus with the Dowager Empress, when they came to tell us the Prince of Orange was back from the military colonies and that they were going for a family drive. Prince

Gagarin was annoyed at having had to wait so long for nothing, all the more so because the Empress had told us to keep together till her return. So he sent for the *lineikas* and put us in them, but fifteen minutes later a heavy shower sent us home soaked. Everyone rushed off to get ready for supper with the Empress, but when we got back we were told she was not going to appear. However we were forced to stay and listen to stories told by General Chernyshev and M. Goblet, who had come back with the Prince. The general praised the military colonies and their flourishing state to excess, just as the Prince had done in his letters to the Princess, in which he called his footman to bear witness that he had found the crops as fine as those in Belgium. The stories the footman and his colleagues told on their return did not at all confirm this story. They all agreed the crops were poor because of the inferior soil, and that the wretched soldiers were treated with incredible severity.

Sunday, July 17th. There was another grand dinner upstairs. I had pleasant ladies as neighbours and M. Bibikov and Prince Dolgorukii opposite, so I was not bored. The beautiful Mme Alopeus, wife of the Russian Minister in Berlin, was also there together with her daughter, whom I had known at Doberan in 1818 when she was a child, but now she is a pretty young woman. They came back for the evening ball, where the polonaise was not danced so as not to tire the Princess. This was the last ball I attended at Pavlovsk.

Monday, July 18th. Pauline spoke to the Prince about her journey home: she was anxious to leave with me before the Princess, so as to travel more slowly. It was therefore settled that I go with her, an arrangement I much preferred to Mama's first suggestion. At the same time the Prince thanked me as if I were doing him a great service. Our start was fixed for July 23rd from Pavlovsk and the 28th from St Petersburg with a *Feldjaeger* as courier to precede us until we reached Brussels. The two berlines in which we had travelled to Russia with our maids were also given us for ourselves, our maids and one of the Princess's valets. Pauline's footman was to come with us, and the Emperor gave us a farrier from his stables to go with us to the frontier. That evening I went with the Gagarins and some other court people to Pavlovsk fair, much the same as that at Tsarskoe. I won a couple of ugly cups in a lottery. No one would believe that we were off so soon. They did not think it possible to leave before the Peterhof fête.

Wednesday, July 20th. I set out with Mlle Kochetov for Tsarskoe on my campaign of paying calls and begging farewell audiences for Pauline and myself. We began with Mesdemoiselles Valuev, Volkonskii and Glasenapp. The first was not at home but the second undertook to arrange a farewell audience with the reigning Empress. The third showed me the magnificent chapel full of gildings on a lovely lapis-lazuli blue and silver ground, with corresponding columns. Mlle Glasenapp, being in waiting, had to leave us, and Mlle Kochetov took me round the rest of the palace. The ladies are all lodged on the ground floor, the state apartments are on the first. They are antique but very rich, with splendid parquet floors and a great deal of gilding, one room all encrusted with yellow amber, another mother-of-pearl. We went through the room where they were going to dine the following Sunday. A neighbouring room is ornamented with Japanese porcelain vases, another totally Chinese.

We reached the Grand Duchess Elena's apartment when she visits Tsarskoe, which is charming – especially the boudoir. The bedroom columns are blue glass with gold surrounds, and a profusion of mirrors everywhere. On the way back we saw the Dowager Empress's apartment, almost in the centre of the palace. It is handsome but sombre since it looks onto the garden and the big lime trees keep out the light. Lastly we penetrated into the Emperor's antechamber and dining room. We then drove to the Alexander Palace to ask Princess Volkonskii, née Repnin, who is the Mistress of the Robes, to get us a farewell audience with the Grand Duchess Alexandrine.

Thursday, July 21st. Princess Khilkov had long wanted to show me the village of Slavyanka, which belongs to Countess Samoilov, née Pahlen. The village is prettily situated but consists of wooden huts like all the others. Several small cabins on the stream at the bottom of the valley serve as bath-houses. The Russian peasants take two baths a week. A château dominates the village but looks run down and is no longer inhabited. We passed another empty country house, whose owner used to give delightful parties according to Princess Khilkov. We dined and spent the evening with Their Highnesses. There was music and Countess Lieven, the ambassadress to London and General Benckendorff's sister, played. She has an extraordinary talent for the piano.

Friday, July 22nd. The last full day I was to spend at Pavlovsk. I had at least been hoping to breakfast alone with Mama, the only moment of the day they leave us free, but Mlle Sylvestre prevented it. I paid some solitary farewell calls on people I saw daily, such as the Gagarins and the maids of honour. The Princess was expecting a visit from the Emperor and wanted us to take our leave of him in her apartment, but His Majesty let us know that he would call on us the following day at noon. The Dowager Empress having said it would be sad if we did not see Peterhof, the Emperor had had the goodness to give orders for us to go there on the following Monday to see the fountains playing. Their Highnesses dined with us, and it was with sadness that I heard the music play at seven for the last time. At eight we had to go downstairs where the Empress put the little girls with all their friends into the dining room – they said to leave us room to talk, but, I believe, not to be bothered by the noise, especially when the Prince of Saxe-Weimar is of the party. That evening he relieved us of his presence and we played a very quiet game of 'running footman'. The Grand Duchess Elena withdrew before supper, and I was summoned to take leave of her with Pauline in another room. I also said my farewells to the Princesses of Saxe-Weimar and after supper Mama and

Pauline retreated very quickly. I followed them without any more goodbyes, except to the young ladies, all of whom wanted to come and see me once more on the following morning.

Saturday, July 23rd. This day was one of the most tiring for me, and above all for the convalescent Pauline. At ten we called on Countesses Fritsch and Eglofstein, and then on our Princess who was not at home. As we were climbing back upstairs to our apartment we unluckily met the Prince of Saxe-Weimar, who gave us each an arm and insisted on seeing us home. We thought to rid ourselves of him by saying we were going to call on Mlle Kochetov, who lived one floor higher up, but he did not let us go till we reached her door, where we took leave of him. Dear 'Cochette' stripped herself of her little bits of household necessities so as to give us presents. I was given a spoon with her initials and Pauline a tea-caddy. After a moment in our own apartment we were sent for to visit the Dowager Empress, meeting Princess Khilkov and Mme Lunin on the way and saying goodbye to them.

After a short moment of waiting in the Empress's antechamber with M. Villamov we were summoned to her presence, admiring as we passed a table covered with every imaginable fruit. She received us in her boudoir and took us into the Greek Hall alongside, where she often works with her secretaries because it is cooler. She made us sit and said how sorry she was that we were going. Speaking of farewells she asked if we had already been to see old Countess Lieven, whom she praised as she deserved. Next she spoke about Mama and praised her just as much, adding that she was anxious she should stay in waiting on her daughter. She was well aware, she said, that I did not like court life. I answered it was true that I preferred a quiet country life, but the Empress said the two can be reconciled. In her view one is never more alone than in the whirl of social life. I agreed of course, and added it was not perhaps the pleasantest form of solitude. The

Empress then stood up and said goodbye to us in a really touching manner. She gave Pauline her blessing and embraced us one after the other. It was the only time she let us kiss her hand.

Once home they told us that the Princess had returned. No sooner were we with her than the Prince arrived all out of breath to say the Emperor was on his way to call on us, and we must run so as not to keep him waiting. Pauline ran off at once after taking leave of the Princess, but she kept hold of me, enjoining me to write to her during our journey as well as to the Oultremont family. While she kept hold of both my hands and I was listening to her orders, the Prince had got me by the shoulders so as to make me run, for fear of keeping the Emperor waiting. In fact he was just leaving when we got to Pauline's rooms, but a servant called him back in time.

He kissed our hands and sat down in an armchair to the left of where Pauline was sitting on a sofa, and when I took a chair in front of him he asked me to sit on the sofa also, so I was closer to his better ear. He talked of various things for a good quarter of an hour, including the charming neighbourhood of Brussels which he longed to see again. He asked me if I really liked our northern provinces. I answered that I loved them as my native land, but was quite ready to admit that Belgium's beautiful countryside was prettier. We thanked the Emperor for letting us see Peterhof and mentioned the coming celebrations there which were so much talked of. He left us finally after kissing both our hands, and we saw him depart without considering the possibility that this man, so full of health and happiness, so much revered and loved, would no longer be alive in six months' time.[2]

We had at last to think of leaving after saying goodbye also to Mlle Divov. Mlle Kochetov and Prince Cherbatov took

[2] Alexander was neither healthy nor happy, nor was he universally loved outside the court. There were four or more conspiracies against him in the last five years of his reign. As his health declined his religious mysticism increased. When he died in distant Taganrog, the story arose that he had become a hermit in Siberia, Fedor Kuzmich.

us to the carriage and Mama joined us to accompany us to Tsarskoe Selo, where the ladies-in-waiting had invited us to dine by order of the Empress Elizabeth. We stopped at Mlle Valuev's, who at once took Pauline and myself into the Empress's presence. She received us in a very simple room on the palace front. We thought she looked fairly well, wearing muslin with plain gold bracelets as her only jewels, and a straw hat. She sat down with us, talked for some time and then asked if Mama had come with us, on which she said she would like to see her, and herself called a footman to fetch her. Soon after Mama the younger Countess Lieven arrived, covered with jewels. She was with Mlle Valuev, who left us once the Empress had bidden us goodbye. From there we went straight to the Alexander Palace to wait on the Grand Duchess Alexandrine, whom we found sitting in a big armchair and looking very well in a white morning wrap, which suited her perfectly. She talked about her sister, our Princess Frederic, from whom she had only had a few lines since her arrival in the Netherlands, and added it was sad she should have started with a winter in The Hague, since the stay there is so disagreeable.

Back at the palace we dined with Mlles Valuev, Glasenapp and Volkonskii, who do not care for one another at all. When dinner was over Pauline was very anxious to see something of the park at Tsarskoe Selo which she had not seen, so Mlle Valuev got into a landau with the three of us. Because of the bad weather we first visited the farm and then the llama house, where I had never been. The weather was too rainy to drive further, and so we went back to the palace to call on the Princess of Württemberg in her very gloomy apart-ment. We took advantage of the occasion to show Pauline the Colonnade and state apartments, where they were laying the table for the christening dinner the following day. Finally, having taken tea with Mlle Valuev, where M. Everard and Countess Tomatis joined us for the drive to St Petersburg, I said goodbye to Mama in the hope of seeing her once more in town.

Sunday, July 24th. After a rather depressing solitary breakfast in my Winter Palace room I went to the Lutheran church,
and Pauline to hers. That evening we visited the islands with
Countess Tomatis and M. Everard, and stopped at the Elagin
Palace, where the interior is pretty but extremely small.[3] The
iron staircase and apartment floors are covered with cloths to
keep them clean. The garden paths are covered with red sand
which looks very neat but hardly attractive. The view from
a small pavilion roof is inviting, but the land lies very low
and the water everywhere seems very high. On the way back
we passed Krestovskii island, the rendezvous of St Petersburg
merchants. It is covered with firs in summer and belongs to
Princess Belosel'skii.

Monday, July 25th. We left for our visit to Peterhof at half
past eight with M. Everard. Our little postilion fell off twice,
which held us up but did not hurt him much. The road is
charming, with country villas on the left and on the right a
stretch of land that runs down to the gulf, and close to Peterhof the palace of Strelna. Peterhof itself is a large palace with
two wings and several outlying pavilions for courtiers and
diplomats. The palace entrance dominates the park and has a
view over the sea and the splendid fountains.[4]

A general, who is governor of the palace and had been
ordered to do us the honours, met us at the gate. Apart from
Russian he could only speak German, so it fell to me to keep the
conversation going. We were pleased to find a fire lit for us and
the breakfast served, which had been sent from Pavlovsk. We
asked for Mme Buturlin, who arrived at once and did not leave

[3] The classical palace was reconstructed from an earlier house in 1818-22 by
Rossi. Most of the interior was destroyed by fire during the Second World War
and now part of the palace is used for exhibitions.

[4] Peter the Great's plans for the palace and park of Peterhof were laid out by Le
Blond, and the fountains started to play in 1721. The Empress Elizabeth, Peter's
daughter, made alterations to designs by Rastrelli and through the years there
were many further modifications. The Germans looted and blew up part of the
palace and the other buildings, which have since been restored. The fountains are
the work of many noted sculptors, but the golden Samson is a copy of the
original by Kozlovskii, destroyed during the Second World War.

us during all our sightseeing. The Emperor had been full of attention and had sent his personal droshky for us together with a *lineika*, so that Pauline could choose which she preferred. As the weather seemed very uncertain we asked for the droshky, but the governor would not believe so many orders had been given and preparations made for very minor personages like ourselves. He was convinced the Emperor was coming himself, to take him by surprise, and felt obliged to keep the droshky back for His Imperial Majesty. However much I pointed out the Emperor was at the camp [at Krasnoe Selo] and had no thought of coming to Peterhof, our man was so extremely nervous that we let him have his way and, being emboldened by a ray of sunshine breaking through the clouds, we climbed into the *lineika* after breakfasting and tasting the most beautiful fruit I ever saw, the produce of the glasshouses of Peterhof.

Everywhere we saw the preparations for the fête of August 3rd and the illuminations which, with all the fountains, must produce a fairyland effect. I must say I was very sorry I should not be there. Not even the smallest fountain was overlooked for us, and every one was working. The chief beauties were the basin in the centre, where a fountain acts as a curtain between men and women, though I doubt if it is thick enough to serve its purpose, the pyramid which sinks gradually while keeping its shape, the golden mountain, a great staircase with its steps lit from underneath while the water flows above. 'Adam and Eve' and the 'Oak and Fir Tree' were names for other fountains. We also saw Marly, the pavilion where Peter used to spend the autumn. It stands over a pool of carp which swim up at the ringing of a bell so as to get a mouthful. All the borders of the pool can be lit up.

Monplaisir, a little Dutch-style house, was another of Peter's palaces. They show his bed, slippers and even his tavern or *kabak*. The house is just like one of ours. This building and the terrace where it stands has the sea at its feet and suffered terribly from the flood, but everything has been restored. There are plenty of fine trees and one sees big ones in the Peterhof park.

They showed us Kronstadt through a telescope from the terrace. Behind the house you see another wonderful jet of water dating from the days of Peter, and there are practical jokes with which the late Empress Elizabeth used to amuse herself by soaking visitors. Of all we saw that day nothing compares in grandeur with the fountain of Samson killing the lion, from whose throat shoots a jet of water sometimes higher than the palace roof. Several other fountains all around fall into the same basin, and beyond them one sees more fountains and the sea. This is the view we savoured when we first arrived, so we climbed another storey to enjoy it better. The Dowager Empress's apartments are here, and there is a room completely full of portraits of women in all sorts of costumes, painted by a single artist in Elizabeth's reign.[5] Next there comes a dining room and several state apartments. In the Empress's they showed us portraits of Mlle Nelidov and Mme van Hoven, both hard to recognise since they were painted in their earliest youth.

After this we hastened to be off, having warmly thanked the governor and said goodbye to Mme Buturlin, for we were due to call on Mme Naryshkin in her country house, and then go on to dine with Princess Cherbatov. We found the first at table with a throng of people, one of whom turned out to be her doctor, a young man of very unattractive looks. The mere idea of always having a professional Aesculapius opposite me would be enough to put me off. We only stayed there for a few minutes, but the house seemed large and pretty. Princess Cherbatov's house is not so big but very pleasant. She had told us a lot about her grounds but they seemed very paltry and her kitchen garden wretched. Provided she has flowers she does not bother about vegetables. Her cherries were not ripe yet though there were plenty of them on the trees, the tops of which I could almost touch with my hand. Pauline had stood up to this fatiguing excursion very well, and Dr Everard had come with us to form an opinion of her strength.

Tuesday, July 26th. Mama arrived at eleven, having come

[5] Pietro Rotari (1707-62).

[150]

from Pavlovsk with the Dowager Empress and the Princess. The Empress wanted to see how Pauline was getting on. Her Majesty then left, having arranged to meet her daughter at Countess Protasov's. From there they were to go to the Fortress to bid farewell to the Emperor Paul's tomb, and to the Kazan' Cathedral to venerate the icon of the Mother of God. The Princess took Pauline with her and so at last I had a few moments alone with Mama. At about one I went to the Princess's to take leave of her and to escort her to Countess Protasov's, where I saw the Dowager Empress, both Nelidov ladies, Princess Khilkov and M. d'Albedyll. I thanked the Empress in my name and that of Pauline for the presents she had sent us, *sévignés* [jewelled pendants] outlining her name in stones of different colours, and took another tender leave of her. Prince Cherbatov came to dine with us and brought us each a clasp in coloured stone, edged with diamonds, from the Emperor. After dinner we all went to see the Shah of Persia's glass bed which was in the Emperor's apartments. It surpassed the picture I had imagined of it in the glass factory, where I had seen its pieces separately. It was mounted in silver and I sat on its glass steps. The evening passed off quietly with Mama.

Wednesday, July 27th. Both Mama and I were up before eight. I packed her things and then we tried to sell some old clothes to a 'Bukhar'.[6] The Hogguer ladies came once more to see us, and at once Mama set off again for Pavlovsk to go on next day with the Princess to the camp at Krasnoe Selo. I went with her to the carriage, feeling very sad to leave her for at least six weeks. Mlles Glasenapp and Tomatis dined with us, along with Messrs Goblet and Everard, and after dinner we said goodbye to the deserted Hermitage. Pauline and I then paid a farewell visit to the Modènes until about eight, and M. van Heeckeren and Countess Tomatis spent the evening with us.

Thursday, July 28th. Before half past seven we were visited by Countess El'mpt, who had brought a newly married couple into town the night before. She stayed for breakfast, during

[6] A Jew from Bokhara.

which I made the acquaintance of the courier who was to go with us, a M. Wimmer, a man of very good appearance looking a little like the Emperor. He has the rank of lieutenant and speaks German and French as well as Russian. We set out at eight, loaded with provisions, and escorted to the carriage by Countess Tomatis and Messrs Everard and Goblet.

I was leaving St Petersburg with regret. Apart from parting with Mama, we had been too well treated there in every way not to preserve a very pleasant and grateful recollection of the place.

Index of Personal Names

Adlerberg, Countess Julia Fedorovna (1760-1839). Born Baggovut; 'Stats Dama', i.e. senior lady-in-waiting; head of the Smol'ni Institute for girls of noble birth from 1802; countess in her own right, 1835; 107-9, 115

Albedyll, Baron Peter Romanovich (1764-1830). Marshal of the Court to the Empress Mother, Maria Fedorovna: 38, 39, 54, 70, 151

Alexander Pavlovich (1777-1825). Emperor, 1801-25: 18 and *passim*

Alexandra Fedorovna ('Alexandrine'), Grand Duchess (1798-1860). Born Princess Charlotte of Prussia; married (1817) Grand Duke Nicholas Pavlovich, (1796-1855), Emperor of Russia 1825-55: 19, 91, 125, 128, 131, 135, 141, 143, 147

Alexandra Nikolaevna, Grand Duchess (1825-44): 135

Alopeus, Count David Maximovich (1769-1831). Russian Minister in Berlin, 1822; m. Janette Ivanovna von Wenkstern (1785-1869), who m. secondly Prince Pavel Petrovich Lopukhin (1788-1873): 142

Anna Pavlovna, Grand Duchess (1795-1865). M. (1816) William, Prince of Orange (1792-1849), King of Holland, 1840-9: 14-15 and *passim*

Apraksin, Countess Ekaterina Vladimirovna (1768-1854). Born Golitsyn (daughter of Princess 'Moustache'), Moscow hostess. Mentioned in Tolstoy's *War and Peace*: 91, 101

Apraksin, Count Stepan Stepanovich (1747-1827). Moscow magnate, m. to preceding. Mentioned in Tolstoy's *War and Peace*: 101

Arakcheev, Gen. Count Alexei Andreevich (1769-1834). A major influence on the Emperor Alexander I during the years 1815-25. Notorious for his cruelty and harsh administration of the military colonies which he instigated: 18, 20, 117

Baranov, Mlle: 108

Barclay de Tolly, Gen. Count Mikhail Bogdanovich (1761-1818): 59

Bavay, de. ADC to the Prince of Orange, 1824-5; Belgian Cabinet Minister, 1846-7: 25, 34, 35, 65, 68

Bazhenov, Vasilii Ivanovich (1737-99), architect: 55

Belosel'skii, Princess Anna Grigor'evna (1752-1809): 148

Benckendorff, Gen. Count Alexander Khristoforovich (1783-1844). Head of the Third Section under Emperor Nicholas I: 61, 112

Bibikov, General Il'ya Gavrilovich (1794-1867). ADC to the Grand Duke Michael, 1824; General ADC to Emperor Nicholas, 1830; Governor-General of Vilna: 30, 140, 142

Bielke, de. Court Marshal to the Crown Prince of Weimar: 137

Bolvillers, Mme de: 71

Brenna, Vincenzo (?1740-1819), architect: 37n, 56

Buis, Willem (1752-1832). Dutch Minister in Paris, Stockholm and St Petersburg, 1798-1803. Became a Russian subject in 1803 and lived in St Petersburg until his death: 84

Buturlin, Colonel Dmitrii Petrovich (1790-1849), diplomat and library director: 97, 127

Buturlin, Mme: 148, 150

Cameron, Charles (c. 1740-1812), architect: 37n, 55, 130

Canning, Stratford (1786-1880). Viscount, 1852; Envoy to St Petersburg, 1824; Ambassador in Constantinople, 1825-9, 1842-7, 1848-58: 102

Goblet, Albert Joseph (1790–1878). ADC to the Prince of Orange, 1824–5; Belgian Cabinet Minister, 1831, 1832–4, 1843–5: 65, 89, 140, 142, 151, 152

Golitsyn, Princess Evdokiya Ivanovna (1780–1850). Born Izmailov; nicknamed 'La Princesse Nocturne': 67

Golitsyn, Princess Vladimir (Valdemar) (1741–1837). Born Chernyshev; nicknamed 'La Princesse Moustache': 66, 91, 93

Granville, Dr Augustus Bozzi (1783–1872): 23

Grün: 23

Gur'ev, Countess Praskovya Nikolaevna (d. 1830), wife of Dmitrii Alexandrovich Gur'ev (1751–1825), Russian Minister of Finance, 1810–23: 67, 116

Harrach, Countess Auguste von (1800–73). m. (morganatically, 1824) King Frederick William III of Prussia (1770–1840): 68

Heeckeren tot Enkhuize en Beverwaard, Baron Ludwig (1791–1884). Netherlands Minister to St Petersburg, 1823–37: 15–16, 85n, 92, 116, 151

Heeckeren van Kell, Baroness Agatha (1801–62). Of Ruurlo; cousin and correspondent of Cornélie de Wassenaer: 9, 13, 111n, 141

Heeckeren van Kell, Baron Charles (1809–75). Of Ruurlo; brother of preceding; m. (1831) Cornélie de Wassenaer (1799–1850), and (ii) Baroness de Sloet: 9, 10

Heeckeren van Kell, Baroness Julia (1802–82). Of Ruurlo; sister of preceding: 9, 13

Heeckeren van Kell, Baroness Wilhelmina, Countess of Wassenaer (1772–1847): 9 and passim

Heiden-Reinestejn, Count Lodewijk Sigismund (1773–1850). In Dutch Navy, 1782–95; in Russian service from 1795 and commanded the Russian fleet at Navarino, 1827: 84

Hessen-Homburg, Frederick Joseph, Landgrave of: 23

Hesse-Philippsthal-Barchfeld, Prince Ernest-Frederick-William (b. 1789). Took refuge in Russia with his father,

the Landgrave Adolf, in 1798; major-general in the Russian service from 1822: 26

Hogguer, Anna Alexandrovna: 21, 84, 93, 151

Hogguer, Jan Willem, Baron: 20–1

Hogguer, Mlles: 113, 118

Hohenlohe, Prince, diplomat: 85n, 100

Hoven, Mme van: 150

Hummel, Johann Nepomuk (1772–1837), pianist and composer, Kapellmeister at Weimar, 1819–26: 24

Imeritia (Georgia), Queen of: 66

Karamzin, Nikolai Mikhailovich (1776–1826). Historian of Russia; m. as his second wife (1804) Catherine Andreevna Kolyvanov (1780–1851), illegitimate half-sister of the poet Prince Peter Andreevich Vyazemskii (1792–1878): 43–4, 70

Kavelin, Alexander Alexandrovich (1793–1850). ADC to the Grand Duke Nikolai Pavlovich (later Emperor Nicholas I) from 1818; Governor-General of St Petersburg from 1842: 25, 94, 101

Khilkov, Lieut.-Gen. Prince Dmitrii Alexandrovich (b. 1789). Governor of Tula, 1827; m. Princess Elizabeth Grigor'evna Volkonskii at Pavlovsk on 30 May 1825: 115, 122, 123, 128

Khilkov, Princess Elizabeth ('Lise'). Maid of honour to the Dowager Empress: 21, 42, 47, 48, 49, 128, 136, 143, 145, 151

Khilkov, Lieut.-Gen. Prince Stepan Alexandrovich (1776–1854). Uncle of preceding; GOC 1st Guards Uhlan Division: 123

Khovanskii, Princess Catherine Pavlovna (1803–37). Attached to the Dowager Empress; m. (1825) Paul Borisovich Mansurov in: 48, 116

Kochetov, Ekaterina Nikolaevna ('Cochette', b. 1794). Maid of honour to the Dowager Empress: passim

Kozlovskii, Mikhail Ivanovich (1753–1802); 148

Kurakin, Prince Boris Alexeevich (1784–1850): 98

Kutuzov, Gen. Prince Mikhail Illarionovich (1745–1813): 73

[155]

Reinbaud, Dr, Lutheran pastor in St Petersburg, 1824-5: 65, 118

Repnin-Volkonskii, Princess Varvara Alexeevna (1776-1864). Born Razumovskii. Mistress of the Robes to the Grand Duchess (later Empress) Alexandra Fedorovna: 42

Rinaldi, Antonio (?1710-94), architect: 37n, 55-6

Romberg, Bernhard Heinrich (1767-1841), 'cellist. He and his two children, Bernhardine (1803-78), concert singer, and Karl (1811-97), 'cellist, performed together in St Petersburg in 1825: 118

Rossi, Karl Ivanovich (1775-1849), architect: 148n

Rossini, Gioacchino Antonio (1792-1868), composer: 10, 24, 44

Rotari, Pietro Antonio (1707-62), artist: 150n

Ruhle, Dr Ivan Fedorovich (1769-1846). Surgeon to the Dowager Empress Maria Fedorovna; never claimed to be a physician: 53, 128

Samoilov, Count Nikolai Alexandrovich (d. 1842; last of line). m. (1825) Countess Julia Pahlen, q.v.: 43, 45

Saxe-Weimar, Princess Augusta of: 72, 141

Saxe-Weimar, Prince Augustus of: 132

Saxe-Weimar, Charles Augustus, Grand Duke of (1775-1828): 24n, 25

Saxe-Weimar, Charles Frederick, Crown Prince of (1783-1853): 16 and *passim*

Saxe-Weimar, Maria Pavlovna, Grand Duchess of Russia, Crown Princess of (1786-1859). Daughter of the Emperor Paul; m. (1804) Charles Frederick, Hereditary Prince, and from 1828 Grand Duke of Saxe-Weimar: 16 and *passim*

Saxe-Weimar, Princess Marie of: 72, 144

Schlüter, Andreas (1664-1714), architect: 54

Scott, Sir Walter (1771-1832): 10, 45-6

Ségur, Count Louis Philippe de (1753-1820): 125

Shcherbatov, Gen. Prince Alexei Grigor'evich (1776-1848). Attached to the Prince of Orange, 1824-5; Governor-General of Moscow, 1844; m. (i) (1809) Princess Ekaterina Andreevna Vyazemskii (1789-1810); (ii) (1817) Countess Sofiya Stepanovna Apraksin (1798-1885), daughter of Count Stepan Stepanovich Apraksin (q.v.) and Princess Ekaterina Vladimirovna Golitsyn, one of the daughters of the celebrated Princess 'Moustache' Golitsyn, q.v.: 30n and *passim*

Skavronskii, Count Paul Martinovich (1751-93): 43n

Sollohub, Count Alexander Ivanovich (1784-1844). m. Sofiya Ivanovna Arkharov (1791-1854): 66

Sor (Saur), Fernando (1778-1839), Catalan guitarist: 102, 115, 118

Spontini, Gasparo Luigi Pacifico (1774-1851), composer: 26

Starov, Ivan (1745-1808), architect: 55, 109n

Stroganov, Countess Sofiya Vladimirovna (1774-1845). Daughter of Princess 'Moustache' Golitsyn, q.v.: 90-1, 96

Sukhtelen, Count Paul Petrovich (1776-1833). Son of Count Peter Kornilovich (1751-1836), who left the Dutch for the Russian service in 1793. Wounded and captured at Austerlitz, where his celebrated retort to Napoleon was misquoted by Tolstoy in *War and Peace* (Book III, ch. 6): 31

Sylvestre. Mlle. Assistant governess to the daughters of the Prince of Saxe-Weimar: 25, 84, 127, 129, 132, 144

Tatishchev, Mme: 87

Thomon, Thomas de (1760-1813), architect: 114n

Tomatis, Countess, maid of honour: 77, 83, 113, 121, 140, 147-8, 151-2

Trezzini, Domenico (1670-1734), architect: 54, 109n, 119n

Trubetskoi, Prince Nikita Petrovich (1804-86). m. (1825) Alexandra Alexandrovna Nelidov, q.v.: 85n, 133

Tutolmin, Ivan Vasil'evich (1762-1839). Favourite of the Dowager Empress: 71

Uvarov, Count Fedor Petrovich (1773-1824). General-ADC; GOC Guards Corps, 1821: 18

Index of Russian Topographical Names